'As a CEO of a private equity real estate firm, I learned a lot from this book and only wish I had been able to read before I had my current job.'

Matt M. Bronfman – CEO, Jamestown, L.P.

'Philip has penned a highly readable primer illustrated with a mixture of academic research and opinion and the highly relatable catharsis of a fruitful "career" through the echelons of management. *Three Peaks Leadership* may be written with a CEO role in mind, but it should resonate with a much wider audience of individuals progressing through the halls of management, responsibility and the uncertainties that these may provoke.

This is a book that senior managers should retain in the top drawer of the office desk, as barely a day will pass when a situation will not present itself to challenge a business leader. *Three Peaks* may not immediately resolve the problem at hand, nevertheless, in turbulent times a quick scan of the Contents section will help steady the hand on the tiller and afford the reader an opportunity to steer back on course when the elements conspire otherwise.'

Paul Durrant – CEO, Conduit Group

'With more companies realizing they now require a social licence to operate, culture and purpose are essential ingredients for sustainable high performance. *Three Peaks Leadership* provides the clear strategic insights into all those areas of focus that are critical for CEOs to achieve this goal.'

Rod Leaver – CEO, Knight Frank Australia

'As a new leader of a new team, there is so much I am learning from this book: Philip's points on agility, listening, humility and curiosity have resonated with me most.'

Cameron Brownjohn – CEO, Federation Asset Management

T0160394

'*Three Peaks Leadership* is immensely readable... it lays it out simply... for any aspiring or existing CEO, how to be an effective leader and what's par for the course... self-awareness, ability to move forward while making it an inclusive journey as an effective teamleader. Every so often, CEOs tend to be in self-deception mode whether at the foothills or at the summit; this book helps along that journey.'

Yash Misra – CEO, IdeasX

'There are plenty of self-help and professional development books that assume a lot about the reader and about their level of experience. Philip Levinson doesn't make these assumptions, and as a result has produced a book with advice that can be applied to any stage of your career – from a start-up with a team of three, to a CEO of a major company. It's written in a way that's accessible and relevant to a broad audience, with a lifetime of experience to back it up.'

Michael Thompson – Producer, Fear and Greed

'Lev's book is a raw and pragmatic guide to the CEO role, and tackles the complexities of the role with brutal honesty and candour. It's a fantastic guide for any new or aspiring CEO.'

David Blight – former Global CEO, ING Real Estate

Three Peaks Leadership

How to make it as a CEO
(and beyond)

Philip Levinson

First published in Great Britain by Practical Inspiration Publishing, 2021

ISBN   9781788602280 (print)
       9781788602273 (epub)
       9781788602266 (mobi)

Figure 1 drawn by Andrew Pagram of Beehive Illustration.

Practical Inspiration Publishing

MIX
Paper from
responsible sources
FSC
www.fsc.org   FSC® C013604

It is not the critic who counts; not the man who points out how the strong man stumbles, or where the doer of deeds could have done them better. The credit belongs to the man who is actually in the arena, whose face is marred by dust and sweat and blood; who strives valiantly; who errs, who comes short again and again, because there is no effort without error and shortcoming; but who does actually strive to do the deeds; who knows great enthusiasms, the great devotions; who spends himself in a worthy cause; who at the best knows in the end the triumph of high achievement, and who at the worst, if he fails, at least fails while daring greatly, so that his place shall never be with those cold and timid souls who neither know victory nor defeat.

Theodore Roosevelt

Contents

Foreword by Phil Kearns

I N 1992, ON tour with the Wallabies to Ireland and Wales, our skipper Michael Lynagh got injured and had to go home. It was the week before the Welsh test; test week is always intense – it's what you play for. Bob Dwyer, our coach, called me into his room. It's rarely good when you get called to the coach's room as it usually means you are going to get dropped or are about to have a discussion on why 'you are playing so bad'. After the niceties, I said to Bob, 'What's up?' He said, 'I'm making you skipper.'

I was completely overwhelmed. A billion thoughts were running through my head, and at the same time none at all. It was just bizarre but I knew it was a great honour. A great honour to lead these men; a great honour to lead my country; a great honour to uphold the history of the past Wallabies.

A sudden realization came over me: what do I do? Where do I start? What do I say? I had no clue.

I said to Bob, 'What do you want me to do?' and then the words I will never forget from a man I love and I have the ultimate respect for. He said, 'Be yourself and the rest will follow.' He added, 'I've picked you for what you do on the field, on the training paddock and off the field, so just do more of that.'

I've never forgotten it and will take it to my grave and have used it in organizations I have led.

Having said all this, I wish I'd had Philip Levinson's book at the time.

Throughout my career as a sportsman and in business, having someone step up, take the reins and lead has been critical. Done well, it's the difference between winning championships and being slated by the press; between the sustainable growth of a company or the humiliation of going bust.

Yet, while the topic of leadership is much discussed, there is surprisingly little written about *why* people want to take the top job and the 'now what?' moment they might feel when they get there. In this book, Philip delves into what makes someone put up their hand to take responsibility for leading an organization and the wellbeing of its stakeholders – while avoiding some of the most common (and in retrospect, avoidable) mistakes. Based on his own experience, including his own mistakes and lack of knowledge, he chronicles the path from preparing to lead, through performing the role, right up to exiting with grace.

Interspersed with anecdotes from his business and military experiences, interviews with leading business leaders and the latest research, *Three Peaks Leadership* provides an indispensable and practical guide for anyone aspiring to the role of CEO or already facing the maelstrom of daily issues doing the job entails.

We all make mistakes; it's a vital part of trying. Failure is often a precondition to success. What sets the successful apart is the ability to take a step back, have a long, hard, honest look at ourselves and learn from our mistakes. Throughout the book, Philip speaks to the essence of leadership: maintaining a sense of curiosity, asking why – and listening to the answers; watching how decisions unfold when you're feeling exposed to the harsh light of day and trusting our gut that we have the wisdom and experience to make the difference we want to see.

I can certainly relate to what can seem like the impossible balancing act of knowing when to apply those soft skills and when to be tough or making the right judgements in the face of competing claims for attention and resources. It takes teamwork and high-end communication skills. It requires a healthy dose of self-awareness and self-control. It needs a strong sense of values, purpose and direction to keep driving forward. And, when the chips are down, you'll need the presence of mind to take time out to press reset, to be kind to yourself to make you a more rounded leader.

Philip provides a sometimes brutally honest account of his time at the top – warts and all – so that we can all learn from his experiences, and have some idea of where the landmines might be buried in the minefield that is today's corporate environment.

About the author

FORMER NAVAL INTELLIGENCE Officer, Philip Levinson is an Asia-based corporate advisor, CEO mentor and managing partner of Penmount Partners, which provides targeted capital markets and leadership coaching solutions to both publicly listed and private real estate sectors globally.

Philip has held senior roles in real estate, funds management and more recently as CEO of two Singapore Stock Exchange-listed real estate investment trusts (REITs). He has advised clients throughout Asia Pacific, Europe and the United States on a variety of real-estate-focused corporate activities.

He established the presence in Australia of the world's pre-eminent asset management firm, Blackstone, and, most recently, led the IPO of Cromwell European REIT, a €1bn diversified REIT with assets across five European countries and listed in Singapore – the first of its kind in Asia.

Philip remains a serving officer in the Royal Australian Naval Reserve, has been engaged in humanitarian work with Refugee Rescue in Greece, and holds a commercial helicopter licence.

He has recently undertaken several mentoring assignments for founders/CEOs of PropTech-related companies globally.

Acknowledgements

It would be remiss of me not to thank those friends and family who have stood by me during the roller-coaster ride that has been my corporate life to date.

To my sons, Sam and Jack: you have lived through the experiences relayed in the book, and I hope it helps you understand.

To the 'Board of Lev': I really appreciate your counsel, support and non-judgemental critiquing over the years. I couldn't have made it this far without you.

To my mentors, both appointed and unsuspecting: you have all moulded me through advice, example and experience to be able to take on the assignments that form the backbone of this book.

To my interviewees: Phil Kearns AM, RADM Lee Goddard, CSC, Adriana Giotta, John Poynton AO, John Churchill and Samantha Martin-Williams: your insights, shared experiences and advice are inspirational. You really 'walk the talk' in terms of commitment to the ideas you have espoused and your willingness to mentor me through the process of writing a book.

JC: for your guidance, friendship and counsel throughout my CEO career, and at the long board meetings, as well as your willingness to put pen to paper to help craft the message on this endeavour, which has taken it from just a half-baked idea to the bookshelves, I owe you!

Thank you to the team at Spencer Stuart, particularly Tahnoon Pasha, for your inspirational guidance and willingness to get involved in this process. To Egon Zehnder, thank you for allowing me to use examples from your excellent surveys.

Thank you to Helen McKenzie for her initial edits as well as Alison Jones, and the team at Practical Inspiration Publishing for helping me with my ideas in this book and getting the book ready to publish. A special mention to Clare Grist Taylor, who turned a mass of words and pages into something I am proud to call my book; you are a literary alchemist!

Preface

'When you become the final decision maker, everything changes.'

CEO

WHEN I FIRST started working on the idea for this book, I took the opportunity to talk with many of my fellow CEOs about their first moment in the top job. Just about all of them found that they were asking themselves the same question: 'Now that I've got here, what do I do?'

That's the 'Now what?' question.

What most of us didn't understand is that no matter our experience, education and career path, nothing had prepared us for the step up to CEO. We had no idea that at least 30% of the CEO job is *social*, particularly if the organization is a public company. Or that we'd have to operate way beyond the comfort zone of what we'd learnt as a marketeer, financier, operations manager, strategist or however we'd built our careers up to that point. That we'd have to re-learn how to manage our time. And that the pressures on us would test ourselves and those closest to us to the limits.

That's why I've written *Three Peaks Leadership*. I want to share with CEOs – as well as anyone aspiring to the top job – some of the challenges I've faced and the lessons I've learnt on my own journey from that 'Now what?' moment to a successful career as a CEO and beyond. I'm not trying to position myself as an all-seeing, all-knowing expert, nor is the book intended to replace the trial and error we all need to learn and grow. But I know that I could have been much more effective, and sooner, if I'd had access to more and better practical information and guidance. I want to use my own experience – the lessons learnt, opportunities missed and occasional wins – to help aspiring leaders prepare for life as a CEO and to maximize their effectiveness once in the job.

Three Peaks Leadership is intended as a hands-on guide, framework and series of checklists that can be applied at all points along your journey – from thinking ahead, through due diligence around appointment, navigating your first 100 days, running the business, being kind to yourself and, crucially, that all-important future-proofing and your own personal exit strategy. I want to deliver strategies, tools and techniques that will help guide the rest of your career. I hope the book will become an invaluable, dog-eared primer that sits in a corner of your desk over the course of a long and successful CEO career.

I've chosen to be your guide on this journey because, having graduated as a lawyer and worked in real estate and finance throughout the Asia Pacific, I've been fortunate to have worked for some truly inspirational organizations and leaders. I have been guided and mentored by the best in the industry – and also learnt first-hand the impact of some truly awful leadership. I've also had the privilege of serving for 20 years as an officer in the Royal Australian Naval Reserve, which provided invaluable lessons in leadership, sacrifice, loyalty and honour.

Along the way, I have experienced discrimination on account of my faith, but that pales into insignificance when compared with the bias – both conscious and unconscious – against women, people of colour and the LGBT community when in the race to the top. As we'll see in Chapter 1, the fact that most CEOs are drawn from the ranks of the socially and educationally privileged does not mean that they are the most suitable for the job; just that they are – for now, at least – the most obvious choice. I want this book to act as a clarion call to, and provide pointers for, *all* aspiring CEOs, whatever their backgrounds.

Leadership is about giving people and organizations what they need, not necessarily what they want. It is about 'walking the talk', being consistent, taking charge and not taking credit, eating last and looking after your people. It is about knowing your business, but not being afraid to ask questions. It's about continuing to develop personally and professionally and ensuring that your people are able to do the same. It can be a joy and a privilege, but it can also be unrelenting, all-consuming and tough.

It is a great honour to be picked to lead a team, but it can also be lonely at the top. You're going to need all the help and support you can muster. You may be in the foothills, or you may already be scaling your first peak, but understanding that those peaks are there to be respected, climbed and conquered every time you take the top job is the first step to career success and fulfilment.

One of the principles I have espoused as a CEO is just to 'get shit done', completing a task or project, even with less information than I'd ideally like, albeit in a state of imperfection. That is certainly the case with this book. I recognize that this topic could be researched and debated *ad infinitum*. Putting the final full stop to it and pressing send to the publishers was a sublime moment, encouraged to no small degree by a brief chat I had with former Australian Prime Minister, Malcolm Turnbull. When asked what was the secret to writing a book, he said: 'Just finish it… desks around the world are littered with excellent, but half-finished manuscripts that will never see the light of day!'

With that in mind, I would welcome your thoughts as a reader and peer on how this guide can get better and more relevant as business changes and practices evolve. I urge you to contact me at philip.levinson@ceolearnings.com and we can look to incorporate your views in future editions.

But we all need to start somewhere. As the Chinese philosopher, Laozi, said: 'Every journey of a thousand miles begins with a single step.' It's time to take that first step.

Philip Levinson

July 2020

Introduction
The CEO challenge and a Three-Peak solution

'It is unfathomable to me why people want do this [CEO] job.'

Headhunter

BACK IN 2004, a *Harvard Business Review* article by Michael E. Porter, Jay W. Lorsch and Nitin Nohria shone a light on the fact that 'nothing in a leader's background, even running a large business within his company, fully prepares him to be CEO.'[1] The article, which carries the intriguing title *Seven Surprises for New CEOs*, is a no-holds-barred review of the challenges and difficulties the authors had seen the alumni of their Harvard Business School's New CEO Workshop face time and again. Their experience shows that you may not be the only newly minted CEO taken aback by an unexpected and unfamiliar landscape, the demands on your time, the need to make decisions with incomplete information, the sheer weight of new professional relationships. In fact, you are in the majority.

It's worth spending some time with these 'surprises', because they offer a sobering summary of exactly why being a CEO is such a tough gig.

---

[1] M. E. Porter, J. W. Lorsch and N. Nohria, 'Seven surprises for new CEOs', *Harvard Business Review*, October 2004. Available from https://hbr.org/2004/10/seven-surprises-for-new-ceos [accessed 18 August 2020].

Surprise 1: You can't run the company

Running the business will be but a small part of the job. One
of the biggest surprises facing new CEOs is the sheer volume
and intensity of *external* demands (shareholders; analyst meeting;
media responsibilities; industry groups; external directorships),
and the need to get to grips with skills like investor relations and
regulation. At the same time, the volume of internal demands
also grows. It's easy to feel that you have lost touch with – or
failed in the first place to get in touch with – the day-to-day
operations of your organization. It's often a hard lesson for a
senior leader who might previously have prided him or herself on
that connection, but a CEO has to let go of a lot of responsibility,
both in terms of operating the company and knowing what's
going on in it. You simply can't monitor everyone and everything.
You may have the final say, but you'll have to learn to rely on
others to advise and implement along the way. As Porter, Lorsch
and Nohria note, influence has to move from direct to indirect
means: 'articulating and communicating a clear, easily understood
strategy; institutionalizing rigorous structures and processes to
guide, inform, and reward; and setting values and tone'.[2] That's
quite a shift.

Surprise 2: Giving orders is very costly

You may have more power than you've ever had before, but you
also have more power to trigger resentment and defensiveness
in colleagues and subordinates; to demoralize and demotivate; to
make mistakes when overruling decisions; or inadvertently set in
train unworkable and unwieldy processes and procedures which
actually slow progress – and sap your energy too. Direct power
should be used only selectively and carefully, *indirect* power is your

---

[2] Porter, Lorsch and Nohria, 'Seven surprises for new CEOs'.

route to success: as Porter, Lorsch and Nohria argue, 'The most powerful CEOs expand the power of those around them.'[3]

Surprise 3: It is hard to know what is really going on

Reliable information can be hard to come by as a CEO. It's generally been filtered before it reaches you, and no one wants to give you bad news. You'll have the tricky balance of finding reliable sources of information throughout the organization – and/or finding it from external sources and advisors – without undermining your senior colleagues. Assume that everyone around you is being economical with the truth or adapting the message to show themselves in a favourable light. You might need to keep digging. It is often not what you're being told that indicates the veracity of information, but the way in which it is being delivered. Be watchful and keep your own counsel and you will soon learn who you can trust.

Surprise 4: You are always sending a message

You'll probably underestimate the extent to which your every move and choice will be scrutinized and interpreted: people will make assumptions about a new CEO's experience and background. Once you are in the job, even the most off-the-cuff remark might be taken as gospel, multiplied and misinterpreted several times over. You'll always be 'on', meeting the challenge of providing consistent messages to a wide range of audiences.

---

[3] Porter, Lorsch and Nohria, 'Seven surprises for new CEOs'.

Surprise 5: You are not the boss

Yes, you've reached the top of the management hierarchy, but you'll still report to a board, and have those shareholders to consider. Managing upwards is still a big deal and can be very time-consuming.

Surprise 6: Pleasing shareholders is not the goal

Porter, Lorsch and Nohria note that 'defining one's goal as shareholder approval may not be in the company's best interest.'[4] The pressures of short-term shareholder value might be acute, but CEOs have to think above and beyond those immediate pressures to create sustainable economic value.

Surprise 7: You are still only human

It's hard to come to terms with the fact that you won't be able to do everything you might want to as CEO, and that you're not the all-conquering superhero CEOs are often expected to be. Having a life outside work becomes more difficult, and relationships with family and friends might change. Staying humble might be a challenge when all around you are looking up to you. But you really are still only human.

Scary stuff, right? Perhaps it's hardly surprising that the average length of tenure for CEOs tends to hover at or below five years. But looked at another way, the seven surprises provide an interesting starting point, a reminder of the constraints under which every CEO has to operate, the balance and finesse needed

---

[4] Porter, Lorsch and Nohria, 'Seven surprises for new CEOs'.

to operate at the top level, and the tricky transitions even the most talented candidates for the top will have to face.

Many of these key themes – the need to work indirectly through a trusted team; the importance of vision; the need for self-care – will be covered in more detail later in the book. For now, we're going to introduce a framework to help you navigate these often-choppy waters: the Three Peaks Leadership Model.

Introducing Three Peaks Leadership

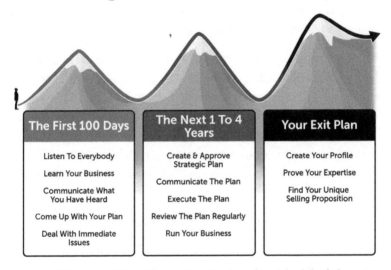

Figure 1: The Three Peaks Leadership Model

The Three Peaks model is designed to help you acknowledge and master the inevitable highs and lows of your term as a CEO, create winning situations for both the company and yourself during your tenure, and also ensure that you exit gracefully, leaving behind a resilient company in good shape, equipped for the vagaries of these turbulent times.

It's not intended as a silver bullet, but it will prepare you for the myriad of issues you will be confronted with daily, and to deal with the whipsaw of interests that compete for your time.

Remember: as CEO, whatever surprises are in store for you, you are responsible for everything that happens in the company, whether you had anything to do with it or not. As the 2020 Covid-19 pandemic demonstrated, external events and trends will impact and affect your daily activities, as well as your company's financial health. You might be told, 'Don't look at the share price – it's irrelevant to your day-to-day job of running the company,' but if and when that share price goes down, you'll still be blamed for it. Just as soon as you think everything is stable, you've dealt with all the issues facing you at a particular moment, you're confident that your people are happy, and you have made all the changes you need to make – somebody falls off a roof, something will happen to derail even the best-laid plans.

Because you're in charge, you have to be able to handle whatever is thrown at you, while at the same time recognizing that each situation will be different and will require a specific, appropriate response. It is your job to ensure that your staff are trained, briefed and secure in their handling of the operations most relevant to them. You need a crisis action plan that's clear, actionable and has been tested. In short, you need a route map and guide to the terrain ahead.

That's what the Three Peaks model is designed to do.

Based on the life-cycle of an average CEO tenure, the model breaks down into four parts:

1. The foothills

Many CEOs find themselves in position without having thought about how prepared they are for this type of role, both in terms of experience and psychological preparedness; nor are they aware of the implications of reaching their goal. On the basis that the best way to start is before you start, we'll be spending time in the foothills, understanding and sizing up the challenges ahead, keeping an eye on due diligence and getting fighting fit for the journey ahead.

2. The first 100 days

Leaders often talk about the first 100 days in office, and with good reason. This is your honeymoon period, when your board, investors, the media and your people will cut you some slack. We'll teach you how to use it to tackle those tasks and issues that will otherwise get harder to achieve the longer you wait.

3. Years 1–3

This is the 'meat' of your tenure when, having tackled any immediate issues and got your feet under the table, you'll be in a position to do some serious planning and implementation. This is the time when you'll need strategic nous and the right team to create, communicate and deliver your vision for your organization.

4. An exit plan – for you and the business

It may seem strange to be talking about leaving a business before you've even started your new role, but we already know that CEOs have a short shelf life. It's crucial that you build into your plans a strategy that positions you well for your next role, while also creating a succession plan and instituting the future-proofing the business will need to continue without you.

The chapters that follow reflect the four stages of the model, guiding you with no-nonsense, practical tips and techniques.

Ready? Then let's begin.

Part 1

In the foothills

1

Looking Ahead: The CEO Role

'…today's CEOs still have to accomplish everything their predecessors did—but in a more complex and public-facing environment.'

Heidrick & Struggles,
Route to the Top, 2019

MEET ADRIANA GIOTTA, clinical psychologist, in-depth coach and thinker. We'll be hearing from her throughout the book. As a CEO coach, advisor and supporter, she knows a thing or two about the role and the people who take it on. Like our headhunter who sees the job as 'unfathomable', Giotta is similarly blunt: 'It is the impossible role. The CEO, just like the politician, will always be the scapegoat, the one to blame for anything that goes wrong and things will go wrong. It is a difficult job.'

So who are these people who continue to aspire to, and succeed in, the top job, why do they do it and, when they get there, what do they do all day?

For Giotta, it's hard to generalize about CEO motivation: it depends on what kind of CEO we are talking about, what kind of organization, its vision. Some are motivated by a sense of social responsibility, a wider purpose or to create good outcomes for people. But, despite all the talk of servant leadership, she has identified that most CEOs like to be in control, and are keen to acquire power, status, visibility and authority. CEOs (and would-be CEOs) are ambitious, driven by the desire to achieve.

Tahnoon Pasha, Head of SE Asia Asset & Wealth Management of executive search company Spencer Stuart, is clear about the reasons *not* to be a CEO. You should never want to: be the boss of a lot of people; crave fame and accolades; have the freedom to do what you like (fat chance) or become financially independent. For Pasha: 'The most effective CEOs are the ones who would do the job anyway, without doing it for the money.' As CEO, you are the synthesis, the soul of the organization, and the energy needs to come from you. Successful CEOs have a passion for their industries, a desire to build something that hasn't been built before, to lead their organizations to new and better places.

My story is fairly typical. I had a desire to make a difference with my life and had no idea how to do it. A key motivator in my ambition to become a CEO came with the realization that the people at the top of organizations – government, companies and associations – were typically the ones who made a difference; they got things done. In order to achieve my goals, I needed to get to that level of authority.

I started working life with Jones Lang Wootton, a name brand in global real estate. Having been accepted onto their graduate programme in the UK, I spent the first few years honing my skills as a valuer, an interesting assignment as I was largely regarded as numerically dyslexic. Then I was sent to Australia to work in a recently formed team specializing in new forms of real estate funding structures, now known as real estate investment trusts, or REITs.

At all points during that job and in other subsequent jobs, I continued to keep an eye on the people in the top jobs. Who were they, where had they come from and how were they doing? They say imitation is the highest form of flattery. I found myself adopting some of the traits of those I admired further up the firm's hierarchy. Some of my attempts at emulation were more successful than others. At one point, I took to wearing the same type of striped shirts as a highly regarded senior partner. Maybe I went too far. One day, before an important meeting, the same senior partner called me into his office and said: 'Go home and change your shirt. We don't need you here looking like a fucking deck chair!'

As my career progressed, I was drawn to observing the people at the top of a company. I was particularly interested in the tone set by the CEO. Unfortunately, I often found it was deficient, with few signs of leadership and accountability. Decisions were taken on the fly and reversed just as quickly; leaders were absent when major events took place. It became clear that not all CEOs were masters in leadership.

I was incredibly fortunate to have the 'light shined on me', to be viewed by senior leaders as having potential, a trait I largely squandered in my first years in business. They mentored me informally, providing guidance and support and in many cases putting up with my antics. My first boss, known to all by his initials CAJD, called me into his office one day to present yet another letter of complaint, this one for mistakenly siting a *For Sale* sign in a churchyard which was diagonally opposite the industrial building we were selling. 'I have a file of these things,' he said, 'You are a total moron!' I found out many years later that he would present these letters to his partners at their monthly lunches to the amusement of all. It was CAJD who provided a firm but compassionate hand that steadied me and set me up for the rest of my career. You need to seek out, and learn from, leaders like this.

Eventually, I figured that observation was not enough. I had some prior military experience, and thought that joining the Royal Australian Naval Reserve might give me the insight into leadership that my workplace was lacking. I was right. Throughout my Navy service, I have actively sought out great leaders and badgered them to allow me to accompany them to sea or on operations, to see first-hand their leadership in action. I ended up serving in the First Gulf War and on a variety of operations, seeing some extraordinary things that I would never have otherwise experienced. It was tough, but it taught me important lessons about self-reliance, perseverance and that it is possible to plumb personal depths and find a way to make the best of situations – life-changing lessons that inform my own leadership to this day.

Two common ways to become a CEO – and their pitfalls

When a business is first starting up, the founder will, by default, be its first 'CEO'. In the early days, when the business is small enough for a direct chain of command and the founder's energy can be at the root of everything, that's fine. The problem comes when a company reaches the size of having, say, 40–50 employees and, for the first time, the founder needs to take a step back and accept that she or he can't manage everything.

Some founders are brilliantly able to manage this transition to delegated management. I was fortunate to work with Steve Schwarzman at Blackstone, an archetypal founder-CEO who was the living – and successful – embodiment of the business. More recently, working with start-ups, it's become clear to me that many visionary founders do not also have the skills needed to be a successful CEO. If this sounds like you, recognize it and delegate the role as soon as you can to someone more suited to hands-on management and leadership.

It's also very common for organizations to make the mistake that their star performers – that stellar salesperson; the marketing whizz – will also make the best CEOs. This isn't necessarily the case. As you will learn throughout this book, the qualities you need to succeed as CEO aren't necessarily the same ones that might have built your career to date. Experience and expertise in one functional area can be a great starting point, but they are only that.

In either case, it might be as well to bear in mind the title of the famous book by top executive coach, Marshall Goldsmith: *What Got You Here Won't Get You There*. That's why you need a plan to prepare yourself for taking the top job.

What do CEOs do?

In 2006, Harvard Business School professors, Michael Porter and Nitin Nohria, asked participants in their CEO Workshop to track how they used their time over a 13-week period. In total, the data summarized how 37 CEOs (35 men and two women) spent a total of nearly 60,000 hours. These numbers alone reflect the imbalance that we all need to redress, if we are to lead more diverse companies that properly reflect positive changes in society.

Porter and Nohria's findings[1] confirm the all-consuming nature of the role: the leaders they studied worked, on average, 9.7 hours on weekdays, conducting business on 79% of their weekends and on 70% of days when they were supposedly on holiday. They spent 47% of their time at company headquarters, with the rest spent travelling, at other company locations and at external meetings.

---

[1] M. Porter and N. Nohria, 'How CEOs manage time', *Harvard Business Review*, July–August 2018. Available from https://hbr.org/2018/07/the-leaders-calendar [accessed 18 August 2020].

The study also found that a CEO's work is diverse:

- 25% of their work was spent on people and relationships;
- 25% on functional and business unit reviews;
- 16% on organization and culture;
- 21% on strategy.

Only 3% of their work was spent on professional development, and fortunately only 1% on crisis management, given how time-consuming and critical this is. Over this period, the sample CEOs were spending 4% of their work on mergers and acquisitions, and another 4% on operating plans.

Face-to-face interactions took up 61% of the CEOs' work time, with the rest split between phone and e-comms. This means a lot of time spent in meetings, although the study also noted the importance of making space for more spontaneous personal interaction and access. Unsurprisingly, it was hard for most CEOs to find the time they needed to be alone to reflect and prepare for time and meetings with others.

Because they oversee a large number of organizational units and work streams and countless types of decisions, CEOs have no choice but to rely on direct reports and work to an agenda – yet 36% of their time, on average, was spent reacting to unfolding issues, both internal and external. Most of them had spent at least some time dealing with a full-blown crisis, the type of situation where visibility and presence, rather than delegation, is required.

While CEOs can't possibly do everything themselves, they still need to make sure they put in place, and monitor, the structures and processes that mean that everyone else can do their jobs to deliver on strategy and build organizational capability – what Porter and Nohria call 'broad integrating mechanisms'.

And then there are the external pressures: boards, investors, suppliers, consultants, industry groups, the media. It seems that everyone wants a piece of a CEO's time. For Tahnoon Pasha, being a CEO can be one of the most constrained roles you can have, especially in a highly regulated environment. There are always stakeholders knocking at your door.

Bearing everything in mind, it's perhaps not surprising that the authors of the study concluded that: 'the sheer complexity of their role—the myriad types of work, activities, and constituencies—is much greater than has previously been documented or perhaps even understood.' They also concluded that a CEO's work involves six dimensions of influence, each posing an apparent contradiction that needs to be balanced each and every day.

DIRECT	INDIRECT
The CEO is directly involved in numerous agendas and makes many decisions.	The CEO also exerts much influence over the work of others, using integrative mechanisms, processes, structures, and norms.
INTERNAL	**EXTERNAL**
The CEO works with the senior team and with employees at all other levels to get all the organization's work done.	The CEO also engages myriad external constituencies, serving as the face of the company, and must bring these external perspectives to the organization.
PROACTIVE	**REACTIVE**
The CEO must articulate a sense of purpose, have a forward-looking vision, and lead the company to greater success.	The CEO must also respond to events as they unfold, from daily issues to full-blown crises that will prove to have a major impact on the company's success.
LEVERAGE	**CONSTRAINTS**
CEOs' position and control of resources give them immense clout.	CEOs are constrained by the need to build buy-in, bring others along, and send the right message.

TANGIBLE	SYMBOLIC
The CEO makes many decisions about concrete things like strategic direction, structure, resource allocation, and the selection of key people.	Much of CEOs' influence proves to be intangible and symbolic; their actions set the tone, communicate norms, shape values, and provide meaning.
POWER	**LEGITIMACY**
CEOs hold formal power and authority in the company that is reinforced by their competence and track record.	CEOs' influence also rests on legitimacy that comes from their character and the trust they earn from employees through their demonstrated values, fairness, and commitment to the organization.

Figure 2: Six dimensions of CEO influence[2]

This balance speaks to the heart of the challenge of being a CEO. It's difficult to do well. Not for the faint-hearted. So, who tends to take it on and what are they like?

What makes a CEO?

There is, of course, no stereotypical CEO, but it is possible to identify some common characteristics. The 2019 Heidrick & Struggles *Route to the Top*[3] survey offers some fascinating insights.

---

[2] M. Porter and N. Nohria, 'How CEOs manage time', *Harvard Business Review*, July–August 2018. Available from https://hbr.org/2018/07/the-leaders-calendar [accessed 18 August 2020].

[3] Heidrick & Struggles, *Route to the Top 2019*. Available from www.heidrick.com/Knowledge-Center/Publication/Route_to_the_Top_2019 [accessed 18 August 2020].

On average, CEOs tend to be around 50 years old on appointment. The vast majority have at least one degree, more often two, frequently from a top university. Most have worked their way up the hierarchy, operating at director or senior levels before being appointed, despite the prominence of a few rapid-growth start-up, often tech-based, companies led by founders with limited wider business experience. Prior senior experience, especially as a CEO elsewhere, or as a Chief Financial or Operating Officer, still seems to matter. Most CEOs are promoted from within their companies. And most are still white men. Despite the obvious and well-documented benefits of board diversity, in 2020, just 37 (7.4%) of the US's Fortune 500 companies were run by women.

Profile and gravitas are seen as important, given that the CEO is both the public and internal face of the organization. Fundamental to the role is the ability to inspire people, to have the confidence to know what it takes to lead and to ensure that it is future-proofed to meet unforeseen challenges.

Knowing these characteristics, however, does not mean that these 'typical' CEOs are successful in leading their companies. For over a decade, the CEO Genome Project has been identifying the specific attributes that differentiate high-performing CEOs, building and analysing a database of information about each leader's career history, business results and – crucially – their behaviours. In a 2017 article in the *Harvard Business Review*,[4] the researchers shared some interesting results which should give pause both to boards appointing top roles as well as aspiring CEOs themselves.

For example, a lack of education pedigree seems to be no barrier to success. While recruiters often tend to choose charismatic extroverts, introverts are slightly more likely to surpass the expectations of

---

[4] E. L. Botelho, K. R. Powell, S. Kincaid and D. Wang, 'What sets successful CEOs apart', *Harvard Business Review*, May–June 2017. Available from https://hbr.org/2017/05/what-sets-successful-ceos-apart [accessed 18 August 2020].

their boards and investors. High confidence might increase your chances of being appointed but provides no guarantee of top performance once in the job. Scarily, although almost half of CEO candidates had worked for companies that had experienced at least one significant or costly blow-up on their watch, this seemed to pose no barrier to them finding another CEO role.

As well as identifying this mismatch between what boards seem to be looking for and performance, the Project also identified four CEO behaviours that prove critical to their performance:

1. They consistently make decisions earlier, faster, and with greater conviction, even amid ambiguity, with incomplete information, and in unfamiliar situations.
2. They balance the priorities of stakeholders with an unrelenting focus on delivering results. They bring others along with them, and have high-end communication and influencing skills but, in the end, they're prepared to make the call.
3. They adapt proactively, focus on the long term and treat their setbacks as opportunities to learn and grow.
4. They set realistic expectations and deliver reliably.

So, put aside any assumptions you might have about fixed traits and pedigrees. There is no one-size-fits-all when it comes to being a CEO. But the CEO Genome Project shows that there are things you can consider and do as you prepare for the top job. The things you do, and the way you do them, will improve the chances of success once you get there.

Samantha Martin-Williams: Good boss versus bad boss

Ex-CEO Samantha Martin-Williams has been around boards and senior leaders for years. I spoke to her when writing this book because I wanted to hear from a senior woman in business, and from someone whom I knew we could all learn from. She has some interesting views about what makes a good boss versus a bad one.

Treating people as individuals

Martin-Williams tells of a great boss she once had who shared his view that behaviours and talent are like blood types: they cut across the superficial differences of race, sex and age and capture the crucial uniqueness of each person. The best bosses do not try to change a person's style, but take a genuine interest in really getting to know it, and then work out how best to deploy it to maximum advantage.

This means getting to know your people: how they think, how they build relationships, how altruistic they are, how patient they can be, how much of an expert they need to be, what drives them, what challenges them and what their goals are. As we've already seen, a leader's most precious resource is time, and a good boss knows that the most effective way to invest their time is to identify exactly how each employee is different and then work out how best to incorporate their idiosyncrasies into the overall strategy.

Leadership, then, is about creating an environment where the unique contribution, the unique needs and the unique style of each employee can be on show.

Creating a level playing field

Great bosses establish company-wide, clear and consistent criteria to reduce bias in staffing decisions and performance reviews. We know that companies that create equal opportunities for advancement have great organizational cultures and stronger bottom lines. It's important that women and other disadvantaged groups have equal access to the right people and opportunities that fast-track careers, and are not lumbered with stereotypical tasks, for example, women doing 'office housework' like running events. Leaders who are clear and unequivocal about diversity and inclusion, and who genuinely believe in fairness, equity and the development of talent – whatever its source – can make a real difference.

Tackling the gender pay gap

The gender pay gap affects women throughout their careers. On average, whatever the sector and wherever in the world, women are paid less than men and, if you break it down by race and ethnicity, the pay gap is even worse.

For Samantha Martin-Williams, closing the pay gap is not just the right thing for companies to do; it is also the smart thing for companies to do. Here are some practical steps you can take to mind the gap:

Gather the data

Pay audits are now mandated in some countries, like for gender in the UK, and with good reason. Best practice in pay parity starts by conducting a simple pay audit. Awareness is the first step to unravelling the issue.

Instil fairness and be aware of bias

Make sure hiring and promotions are fair by auditing reviews and promotions regularly to check you're not systematically rating men more highly and promoting them more quickly. Train managers to understand the impact of gender bias on decision-making.

Establish the right framework and culture

You need a well-communicated framework which makes clear expectations when setting consistent criteria for hiring and promotions. This will help to set the right culture around equal opportunities.

Make it standard for women to negotiate

Women often feel less able to negotiate their pay than men, so organizations need to set a clear tone from the top that they'll be encouraged and supported to actively develop the skills associated with negotiation.

A culture of sponsorship

Sponsors who support individuals' career development and advocate for them make a real difference. These are people in authority who can drive and mould workplace cultures, leading by example, taking an active role in talent management. They practise other-focused leadership rather than self-focused leadership, understanding that helping others to make the most of themselves creates competitive advantage and business success.

And what makes a bad boss? Martin-Williams is unequivocal: everyone dreads a micro-manager. Micro-managers can be extremely common in workplaces but are usually unaware that they are micro-managing. It's a behaviour often driven by personality, which makes it very hard to turn off. Its downsides are obvious: smothering staff self-determination, creativity and morale can only negatively affect productivity. You'll also lose your best talent, who will back themselves and leave.

2

Looking Ahead:
Start Before You Start

'As CEO, I need the capacity to transform myself as well as my organization.'

Respondent,
Egon Zehnder CEO survey, 2018

THIS QUOTE, FROM a respondent to the 2018 CEO survey[1] by executive search consultants, Egon Zehnder, speaks to an essential truth about the top job: your CEO journey starts long before you take your seat at a board table. If you have decided that being a CEO is your goal, then get ready for years of work, preparation and perseverance. It is not for everyone but, if you are up for a challenge, enjoy learning and know how to – when necessary – fly by the seat of your pants, then get set for the expedition of your life.

Getting the job is, in fact, the easy bit – provided you've laid the groundwork. Before you find yourself on a headhunter's shortlist, there's plenty to do apart from simply building your technical skills and experience. You'll also need to concentrate on observation, positioning, participation, building your career in a way that will

---

[1] Egon Zehnder, *The CEO: A personal reflection*, 2018. Available from www.egonzehnder.com/CEO-study-2018 [accessed 18 August 2020].

prepare you to make the transition to CEO. And you'll need a healthy dose of self-awareness and self-reflection along the way, not to mention perseverance.

Laying that groundwork in advance is crucial. By the time you land a CEO job, the chances are that you'll be too busy getting to grips with the organization and the job to learn new skills. You'll also find it harder to carve out time to reflect on your personal development. It stands to reason then that the period before CEOs take control is the best time to assess yourself, fill any critical weaknesses and build your skills base.

You can start this the day you walk into your first job. Look at the top of the organization and decide whether the person in the CEO role is someone you would like to emulate. If you decide that they are, then the die is cast. You seek to learn what they did to get there, how they positioned themselves: did they found the company? Did they work their way to the top or were they brought in? What are their special skills and how are they regarded by the staff? Answering these questions can help you to devise your own plan; it can provide a roadmap to the top job.

My first CEO role came about because I was known in the market; I had a suitable profile and the requisite experience. I was known to the right people and had the market insight to know that the incumbent CEO wanted to leave.

As you contemplate your first peak, position yourself in your chosen field in such a way that when a suitable CEO role comes up you are visible to those seeking candidates and ready if you are fortunate enough to get the job. Participate in and contribute to your industry. Become a thought leader, learn your craft, surround yourself with people whose approach and experience complements yours. In my case, I wrote chapters on REITS for industry publications and joined Australia's leading property association, working my way up to their board as Chairman of a committee. Attend industry functions and events, but always keep your eyes on the prize. Establish your reputation and gravitas among your industry associates.

Consider moving jobs to increase your visibility and footprint – without being seen as a job hopper, but as someone with a clearly defined path to success. Cultivate relationships with headhunters and always be deferential. If they phone you to talk about a role and you find that it is not for you, suggest candidates who may be more suitable and, if necessary, arrange introductions. Be generous with your contacts. It might not pay dividends for years, but you may find at some point that a headhunter with whom you've developed a relationship is gatekeeper to a role you really want and are totally suited for. Canvas the headhunter's views on why you did not make the short, or even the long list, for a job and take their advice on board.

One headhunter I encountered earlier in my career made the point that over 50% of board seats are awarded to people they know and trust. His blunt advice? 'Get the fuck out of my office, network with your peers, build a contact base, set yourself up for success and then come back to see me.'

Strategies for the top

Suzanne Bates, author and CEO of leadership advisory firm, Bates, has many years' experience of working with CEOs and aspiring leaders. In a 2019 article,[2] she identified seven key strategies for leaders aiming at a CEO role, particularly those in-house candidates who so often seem to get the job (see Chapter 1). Bates believes that adopting these strategies sooner rather than

---

[2] S. Bates, '7 strategies for becoming CEO: How to position yourself for the top job', *Bates*, 17 January 2019. www.bates-communications.com/bates-blog/7-strategies-for-becoming-ceo-how-to-position-yourself-for-the-top-job [accessed 18 August 2020].

later can make a real difference to being 'CEO ready' – or as ready as you can be. They provide a great checklist for anyone in the foothills.

1. Establish your 'why'

Answering why you want to become a CEO can be surprisingly tricky. After all, as we've seen already, it's a job that comes with huge responsibilities and emotional burden. But, for Bates, it's essential to reflect on your own 'why', a personal answer to the question beyond your vision for the company, however related that might be. She suggests a bit of time travel to help you work this out: imagine yourself five years into the job. Think about what's changed; what's better; what are your proud of; how is the company different; how are *you* different? You may find it useful to go through this exercise with your coach or advisor.

2. Build a compelling vision

Assess the landscape of your industry, develop a clear idea of what the future could hold, and consider the types of moves you would make to position the company for success in the next five to ten years. Other qualities are also important: are you flexible, curious and agile? Are you able to make decisions when you don't have all the answers? Do you have conviction without arrogance? Vision plus character is a winning formula.

3. Be a leader of people

Leaders who achieve long-term success get results and develop their people. And, according to a 2019 Bates survey, leadership qualities like authenticity and integrity correlate more closely with high growth than more obvious leadership traits like confidence and assertiveness. Winning leaders inspire people to get outstanding results because others admire them and trust their character. They can be tough and still win others' trust and best efforts, because they are reliable, truthful, real, sincere, genuine and transparent in their interactions.

4. Establish a kitchen cabinet

Building and maintaining peer relationships as you progress in your career is crucial. Working with a coach can also really help. A confidential network like this – a 'kitchen cabinet' – can help broaden your thinking, and provide some much-needed perspective; external and internal supporters will educate you, tell you the truth and help you to keep it real. We'll be returning to this theme in Chapter 3.

5. Embrace your development

Investing time in learning and being open to change are, according to Bates, a sure-fire indicator of successful leaders. The best leaders also know that 'what got them here won't keep them there'. Never skimp on your own development.

6. Get to know the board of directors

One for those prospective internal candidates: take every opportunity you can to get exposure to the board, inside and outside the boardroom. External candidates should also do their homework as soon as they have a job in their sights. Remember that exposure to other boards and how they work is also valuable.

7. Live your leadership values

What have you learnt along the way as a leader and how? What have your experiences taught you about life, about people, about business, about the world? As CEO, you need to stand for something, and people need to know what you believe in. Look at your own career to date and think about the values that have shaped you. Think about stories from your life and career that define you.

What does an executive search firm look for in a CEO candidate?

These are the top selection criteria used by Tahnoon Pasha, Head of SE Asia Asset & Wealth Management of executive search firm Spencer Stuart, when identifying and assessing candidates for CEO roles:

- Track record
- Execution capability
- An informed and distinctive strategic point of view
- The ability to manage partnerships with boards and executive committees
- Emotional intelligence, including resilience in the face of failure, crisis and challenge
- High levels of integrity
- The ability to build strong and effective management teams and harness them to achieve business goals

Pasha believes that you should be planning for your first CEO role at least five years in advance, working on your track record of achievement, building your profile and developing your network.

Transformation, reflection and mindset

In the Egon Zehnder CEO survey mentioned above,[3] more than 50% of respondents agreed with the statement 'Transitioning into the role of CEO required an intense period of personal

---

[3] Egon Zehnder, *The CEO: A personal reflection*, 2018. Available from www.egonzehnder.com/CEO-study-2018 [accessed 18 August 2020].

reflection.' By focusing on the *human* side of preparing for, and making the transition to, becoming a CEO – on what it actually *feels like* to take on the responsibility – the survey identifies an often less acknowledged truth about getting ready for leadership. They rightly identify that it's not all about experience, positioning and visibility – important though they are. It's also about what the survey calls 'the critical elements of preparation and adaptation': the need to pause and reflect.

The team at Egon Zehnder talk about CEOs being on a *dual journey*:

> *Being a CEO*: how we embody leadership ourselves; and

> *Doing the job of CEO*: executing the operational requirements of the role.

In the survey, 79% of Chief Executives agreed or strongly agreed that they need the capacity to transform themselves as well as their organization. This means that CEOs have to transform themselves while at the same time transforming the business. It can be a tricky balancing act. The majority of the CEOs in the survey felt they'd developed the skills they needed to do their jobs, but acknowledged the need to focus on *mindset*, a continual growth approach that requires introspection, self-awareness and the ability to adapt.

Carol Dweck's fixed versus growth mindset

Psychologist and bestselling author, Carol Dweck, has written eloquently on the power of adopting a growth rather than a fixed mindset.[4] Dweck's research has led her to believe that one of the most basic beliefs we carry about ourselves has to do with how we view and inhabit what we consider to be

---

[4] C. Dweck, *Mindset*. Robinson, updated edition, 2017.

our personality – and it can have a profound effect on how we behave.

People with a growth mindset believe that our abilities and understanding can be developed, that we can get smarter, more intelligent and more talented through putting in time and effort.

People with a fixed mindset assume that abilities and understanding are relatively fixed. They may not believe that intelligence can be enhanced, and that you either 'have it or you don't' when it comes to abilities and talents.

Not surprisingly, I am firmly of the view that CEOs need a growth mindset to succeed.

The message for aspiring CEOs is clear: you need to get used to working on your own personal development as well as your professional career development.

The Egon Zehnder survey suggests three ways in which we might all open up to personal growth:

1. Be curious and challenge yourself by building and developing teams that are willing and able and which speak truth to power.
2. Adopt personal habits that allow you the time and opportunity to maintain your energy, reflect, and be mindful. You need to be connected with yourself and others.
3. Look outside yourself and your organization for ideas and learn to experiment outside your comfort zone.

We'll be returning to some of these themes in Chapter 3.

It's tough at the top, and it can be lonely. That's why preparing for the *being* side of the role – the human side of leadership – is so crucial.

Developing emotional intelligence

Daniel Goleman, champion of emotional intelligence (EI), is suitably bullish about its power:

> The four domains of Emotional Intelligence – self-awareness, self-management, social awareness, and relationship management – can help a leader face any crisis with lower levels of stress, less emotional reactivity and fewer unintended consequences.[5]

Big claims. But, if it's true that we tend to focus on the *doing* aspects of our leadership rather than the *being* aspects, it stands to reason that it's never too early to pay attention to our emotional as well as our cognitive intelligence.

Goleman's research has led him to believe that successful leaders share a high degree of EI. It's not that he considers IQ and technical skills to be unimportant, but he describes them as 'threshold capabilities' – entry-level requirements for senior roles. But it's EI that makes the difference: 'Without it, a person can have the best training in the world, an incisive, analytical mind, and an endless supply of smart ideas, but he still won't make a great leader'.[6]

In a 2017 *Harvard Business Review* article,[7] Goleman builds on this thesis in an article co-authored by Richard Boyatzis, adding 12

---

[5] D. Goleman, '4 emotional intelligence skills for trying times', Korn Ferry. Available from www.kornferry.com/insights/articles/4-emotional-intelligence-skills-for-trying-times [accessed 18 August 2020].
[6] D. Goleman, 'What makes a leader?' *Harvard Business Review*, January 2004. Available from https://hbr.org/2004/01/what-makes-a-leader [accessed 18 August 2020].
[7] D. Goleman and R. E. Boyatzis, 'Emotional intelligence has 12 elements. Which do you need to work on?' *Harvard Business Review*, 6 February 2017. Available from https://hbr.org/2017/02/emotional-intelligence-has-12-elements-which-do-you-need-to-work-on [accessed 18 August 2020].

EI competencies to his four EI domains. You may be surprised that competencies like empathy and self-control sit side by side with a focus on achievement, the ability to influence or conflict management. That's because we tend to think about EI too narrowly, as something 'sweet and chipper'. It's not. To excel as a leader, you need to build your awareness of all these competencies, and work on those areas where you're perhaps less naturally inclined. Goleman sees honest feedback and coaching as two key means of improving areas of what he calls an 'EI deficit'.

SELF-AWARENESS	SELF-MANAGEMENT	SOCIAL AWARENESS	RELATIONSHIP MANAGEMENT
Emotional self-awareness	Emotional self-control	Empathy	Influence
	Adaptability		Coach and mentor
	Achievement orientation		Conflict management
		Organizational awareness	Teamwork
	Positive outlook		Inspirational leadership

SOURCE MORE THAN SOUND, LLC, 2017 © HBR.ORG

Figure 3: Goleman's emotional intelligence domains and competencies[8]

Self-awareness is key

Goleman himself has gone on record as saying that, of his four EI domains, self-awareness is key. This was reinforced for me in an interview with Rear Admiral Lee Goddard, one of the most inspirational leaders I've ever encountered. Goddard tells the

---

[8] D. Goleman and R. E. Boyatzis, 'Emotional intelligence has 12 elements. Which do you need to work on?' *Harvard Business Review*, 6 February 2017. Available from https://hbr.org/2017/02/emotional-intelligence-has-12-elements-which-do-you-need-to-work-on [accessed 18 August 2020].

story of a valuable piece of advice he was offered early in his career. In 1990, he spent six months at sea as a midshipman, the most junior officer, living among the 'other ranks'. The day before he was promoted to sub-lieutenant, one of his favourite Leading Seamen pulled him aside and said:

> Sir, you are about to become an officer and we will follow you because of the line of command and your authority. Don't doubt we will often criticize you for being an officer, because that is the Australian way. But the moment that you stop behaving and conducting yourself like an officer that is when we will *really* criticize you and we will make you aware of that.

For Goddard, this was invaluable advice he's never forgotten: the perception of those you are leading is paramount. Like Goleman, he believes that the most important leadership attribute is self-awareness. How others perceive you versus how you perceive yourself is absolutely critical.

Grit: Passion and perseverance combined

Psychologist Angela Duckworth opens her bestselling book, *Grit*,[9] with an anecdote about why so many cadets at the US's elite Military Academy at West Point tend to drop out of the programme during the first two months, despite a rigorous selection process. It seems that the key to sticking it out has less to do with talent or natural ability, but more to do with *grit*, defined by Duckworth as the *passion and perseverance* needed to accomplish long-term goals.

The message for new and aspiring CEOs is clear. For Duckworth, no matter how talented you are, if you want to achieve your goals you need to put the work in; in fact, effort counts twice because it not only builds skill, but makes skill productive.

---

[9] A. Duckworth, *Grit*. Scribner, 2016.

Talent × effort = skill

Skill × effort = achievement

Effort, then, is a multiplier, but it also takes time. You need to work at improving your skills consistently, and over time; with grit, it's a marathon, not a sprint.

But perseverance on its own is not enough. If you're in it for the long game, you're going to need *passion* to sustain you along the way. And for that, as Duckworth notes in *Grit*, you need a hierarchy of personal goals, a combination of:

- an overarching vision, a big dream, something that's meaningful to you and that can inspire you for a long time – becoming a CEO, for example; and
- smaller, achievable, goals, to help you get wins, make progress and stay motivated.[10]

In between could be all sorts of mid-level goals, but they all need to be aligned so that you can make decisions along the way about which goals to pursue and which ones to ditch.

Warren Buffett's three-step, 5/25 strategy for life goals

Top investor Warren Buffett's secret to success is intense focus; instead of doing more, he does less.

He once told his pilot that in order to reach his goals, he needed to do three things:

1. Write down his 25 top goals.

2. Circle the top five most important.

3. Separate the top five into their own list, and put goals 6–25 on a 'not to do' list, which should be ignored until he'd achieved his top five.

---

[10] Duckworth, *Grit*, pp. 73–88.

The good news is that Duckworth believes grit can be cultivated. You can make yourself grittier by contemplating her four key characteristics of grit:

Interest

You need to care enough, and be curious about, what you want.

Practice

You won't get better unless you work at it. Make that practice deliberate and intentional, and make it a regular habit. Perhaps you need to build a better professional network, so set aside time each week to think about how you'll build and nurture the right connections on a more regular basis.

Purpose

You need a reason to do what you do. Purpose, according to Duckworth, is 'the idea that what we do matters to people other than ourselves'.[11] As well as a core grit factor, purpose can be a great motivator.

Hope

If you don't think it's possible, you won't try to do it. Grit rests on the expectation that your own efforts can improve your future. This is where the right mindset is so important; as Duckworth says: 'If we stay down, grit loses. If we get up, grit prevails.'[12] A little optimism goes a long way.

As you look ahead to leadership, that's not a bad lesson to bear in mind.

---

[11] Duckworth, *Grit*, p. 175.
[12] Duckworth, *Grit*, p. 109.

3

Fighting Fit:
Resilience and Wellbeing

'…no one is honest anymore… there are very few people you can fully trust. That is the tough part.'

CEO, Egon Zehnder survey, 2018[1]

WHEN I TOOK up my first CEO position, I quickly realized that I needed help. I needed to understand what I didn't know and why. I needed to tap into the experiences of those who had come before me. I was lucky enough to meet my mentor, John Connolly, two days into my appointment. As one of Australia's most influential men, he was the mentor I really needed and he showed up at absolutely the right time.

I had a one-hour AGM presentation to prepare, to be delivered in 15 days' time. One of the things he wanted me to do, as part of my preparation, was to gather all the relevant documentation and information so that I could present cogently and be, not just look, the part in my new role. John walked into the company and said to the Head of Investor Relations: 'Brief me on the company.' At the end of the briefing, he said: 'Brief me on the company; I could have picked up what you've just said from the website. What is

---

[1] Egon Zehnder, *The CEO: A personal reflection*, 2018. Available from www.egonzehnder.com/CEO-study-2018 [accessed 18 August 2020].

the essence of this place? I need you to provide this… now.' He took charge of collecting the right information and prepared me to speak confidently about the results of the company from the previous year. The result was that I was able to communicate a sense that I was a safe pair of hands and that I was in command. It also gave me the self-assurance to stand in front of the business as the right guy for the job.

There is little doubt that leadership can be one of the loneliest places to be. In the Navy the captain dines alone. As the CEO, you are responsible for the lives and safety of everybody under your command. The role puts you in the spotlight, or perhaps more aptly, the searchlight; all eyes are effectively on you from the moment you arrive in the morning until you leave at the end of your day. The constant barrage of concern, criticism, time pressures, immediate issues and strategic direction will be wearing. Your best course of action is to prepare, prepare, prepare. You need to be fighting fit, both mentally and physically, and to have the self-awareness to know when you need help and support.

As CEO, you may be in charge but, as we've discovered, you're still only human. The role is challenging, complex and has the potential to be all-consuming. The stereotypical CEO sleeps for four hours a night, trains for and competes in Ironman events globally, teaches at their MBA alma mater and still manages to serve on numerous government and industry boards while delivering double-digit annual growth.

In reality, while CEOs often are driven, focused, performance-oriented insomniacs, they also have perfectly human failings and insecurities. The problem is that admitting to them may seem to have a detrimental impact on perceived invulnerability and fortitude, lessening authority and worth. In fact, nothing could be further from the truth. The mental and physical wellbeing of the CEO is crucial to the overall health of the business. You need to build the resilience and stamina you'll need at the top.

For Adriana Giotta, resilience is the psychological ability to pause, an internal process of being aware of oneself and knowing when we need to get ourselves off the hook and take a break and do something that is rejuvenating. This awareness helps us to find our inner equanimity and re-energize. 'Leadership roles are exhausting; there is a need to find the balance between being in the forefront and withdrawing. Once we feel re-energized we can go back into the battlefield and go again.'

I have been flying helicopters for many years. When I get in the cockpit, no one gives a toss whether I'm a CEO or not. I'm judged as a helicopter pilot and on my ability to fly the chopper safely. As a diversion, it consumes me and creates an energy that I can take back into the office. I'm doing an activity that I love and is all-consuming. It makes me step away from the day to day; in Giotta's terms, it 're-energizes' me.

It's all too easy for the nature of the CEO role to overwhelm every aspect of your life. There's a real risk that we become too identified with the role itself and invest everything in it. And that's a dangerous road to go down. For Giotta, if we allow the role to become a persona, an inflated aspect of our personality at the expense of any other, resilience is lost because there isn't anything else at the level of the personality structure. The solution is to not give into that, but instead to continue to invest in other aspects of your personality, including friends, time off, family, children and hobbies: 'This way the CEO will be in a better place to be a CEO.'

It's never too soon to start making this *intentional* investment of time and effort into other aspects of your personality outside work. It will ultimately make you a better leader because you'll have the right habits and a support system; you won't be alone. Self-care is not selfish; it's essential if you're going to face the challenges of being a CEO.

Take care of yourself

Activate the parasympathetic system

The problem with not feeling like you can take time away from your job is that our brains work against us. Too often, stress and conflict will look to trigger our sympathetic nervous system, stimulating a 'fight or flight' response which shuts down all but the most essential of the brain's functions – hardly a fertile environment for leadership and learning. According to Adriana Giotta, to re-energize, we need to activate our parasympathetic nervous system, the 'rest and digest' system associated with wellbeing and the functions of the middle prefrontal cortex, which become shut off when under stress or triggered. When we're in that state, we can rebalance ourselves, re-energize, find stillness and clarity, which makes it easier both to avoid the feeling of being overwhelmed and to find the answers to challenging problems.

Many of us will also have experience of what psychologists call incubation. By taking a break from consciously working on a problem and engaging in an unrelated task, or resting, our thinking is unconsciously re-energized. This is when our brains slip from more focused, active thinking into diffuse mode, where we form connections and sub-consciously mull over problems. We may think that we're taking a break from thinking, but our minds are still working. It's not possible to use both focused and diffuse modes at the same time; we need consciously to alternate between them. Trying to maintain the focused mode for too long is not only impossible and tiring; it can also be counter-productive. Our thinking stagnates and we develop tunnel vision. New ideas won't flow and we often just can't see a way through when we hit an obstacle.

Activities like deep breathing, yoga, meditating, Pilates, things that are very soothing or contemplative, all help to activate our parasympathetic system. Or you might take time out to read or have a bath, go on a quiet walk, have a swim, or set aside some family time. Do whatever works for you, and guard that time jealously.

The mental capacity of the CEO is incredibly important. Many report feelings of being overwhelmed and unable to perform the multitude of tasks that they are charged with. This eventually leads to irrational behaviour, breakdowns in relationships, breakdowns in communication and ultimately a CEO not doing their job.

I used to get told off for going to the 'bear cave', when I was actually trying to isolate myself temporarily in order to find solutions to difficult challenges. You might do something similar so you can calm your mind and be better prepared to deal with those unexpected issues that crop up. If so, explain what you're doing to anyone affected by your behaviour so they understand what's actually going on.

You'll then be able to take better decisions, have more clarity and connect more effectively with your staff.

Keep fit

Like an Olympic athlete who trains for ten years for a minute of glory, the tenure of a CEO requires continuous physical, mental and emotional preparation. Physical exercise will help. Keep fit, ride a bike, go for a run, go to the gym, swim, go paddle boarding – again, do whatever it is that you love doing, and give yourself a routine for exercising regularly. Think about ways of varying your routine when you have to travel and, when the inevitable emergencies and crises get in the way, try to get back to your routine as soon as you can.

Doing whatever it is that brings you joy, whenever you can, will help you to spring back from any setbacks or issues the daily routine throws at you. If you can balance yourself physically, emotionally and mentally to do the job, your mental acuity, decision-making ability and speed of implementation will increase in direct proportion to your physical, emotional and mental wellbeing. Exercising and decompressing the pressure that builds up during the day is essential in order to relieve stress, enhance productivity and improve relationships.

Sleep well and be mindful of your circadian rhythms

Getting deep, relaxing and restful sleep is critical to proper functioning. Become aware of your circadian rhythms. Learn whether you are a morning or an evening person, or even a 'hybrid' (Daniel Pink's book, *When: The Scientific Secrets of Perfect Timing* has some valuable insights on this). When you know your own rhythm, you can plan your day accordingly.

If you are at your best in the morning, make sure that all of your important meetings are held then. If you can, delay decision-making until you are at the peak of your daily cycle and ensure that you don't make any at the nadir.

During my Navy service I was assigned as Liaison Officer to an Admiral who had the entry 'Lima Lima Delta' in his daily run sheet, every day from 16.00 to 18.00 hours. Not being fully aware of all Naval acronyms, I asked him what that stood for and he answered, 'Little Lie Down'. During those two hours, he was not to be disturbed; it was the time he gave himself to recharge and re-energize. He had developed the habit when he was the captain of a ship and found it critical in managing fatigue and looking after his own wellbeing.

If it's good enough for an Admiral; it should be good enough for you.

Breathe

There I was at 500 feet, with a 200 feet-per-minute rate of descent, in a busy circuit, a strong crosswind, trying to land a chopper on a little 'H' with a circle around it, which was bouncing up and down my cockpit windscreen like a fly in a bottle.

As I was working my hands and feet in some semblance of coordination, my instructor suddenly piped up and said, 'sing me a song!'

'I don't sing songs,' I replied.

'Come on, you must know a song,' he retorted. 'Or just sing the alphabet.'

So I did.

Then he said something that has stuck in my mind ever since: 'Mate! By my watch you hadn't taken a breath for 1 minute and 20 seconds. In a few more seconds, you would have blacked out. That wouldn't have worked out well for you and your passengers!'

The moral of the story is that you have to learn to breathe. Recognize that, when you're concentrating hard, you can forget to do it. Watch for the signs and take action to make sure you are always breathing, particularly under stress.

Every morning, before I swiped my entry pass into my office, I would stop and take three deep breaths. After letting the air out from the third breath, I would say 'Remember to breathe!' Then I'd walk onto the floor to start my day.

There are many methods of breath control. I advise you to find one that works for you and use it – every day.

Be kind to yourself

If I wasn't in constant motion, like a shark, I would berate myself for it. I would say to myself: 'You're so lazy! Look – you took an hour out of your day just to relax.' But I learnt that, if your body is telling you that you need to slow down, then you must do it, because there will be consequences if you don't. Learn to accept that the machine will keep going without you. Step back and review what's going on; take some time out and reflect. You don't need to be in perpetual motion; if you are, or try to be, it's going to catch up with you one day.

One of the biggest mistakes I made in one role was to be continuously reacting to everything that happened. I bounced around like a ping-pong ball from one thing to the next. It took me a while to understand how to fully take charge, for the benefit of everyone involved. You won't have enough wriggle room in your schedule to accommodate everything that happens, so something has got to give. Be kind to yourself, cut yourself some slack and make sure you take time out. You may need to leave something in the tank for events that you simply can't foresee.

The right support

While being battered from all sides by internal and external pressures, it's easy to feel overwhelmed, or to doubt yourself. However good your regime of self-care is, you must also accept that you're not an island and at times you'll need to tap into your support network.

Honest feedback

I went into my first CEO job thinking I had to be right most of the time. If I wasn't, then the team would not respect me, the market wouldn't respect me, the board would think I'm an idiot and my tenure would be very short. I'm the guy leading the team; I'm the guy the board has put in place to run the company.

The issue was that I didn't have anybody to gauge whether I was right or not. A CEO, leader or the captain of a ship is surrounded by sycophants. They could say it is night-time and raining when it is daylight and sunny and the people around them would say you are absolutely right (and if in the Navy they would end the sentence with *Sir.*) There may be some dissenting views, but they are not always audible, delivered at the right time or able to survive being quashed on the way up.

We'll be talking more about teams in Part 2. For now, suffice to say that it took me a long time to work out that unless and until you get a team with high levels of mutual trust, nobody is going to provide you with that honest counter-view.

Not having that team cost me dearly. I was encouraged to deal with the players I had inherited and align with their way of playing instead of getting them to adapt to my leadership and the strategy we were putting in place. You need your top team around you, people who are in lockstep and who are aligned with what you believe and what you do. I was able to persuade some of them that whatever I did was done with the best intentions, but that took some time. I worked out that if critical guidance was not going to come from within the company, I would need to put together an external team; I called it the Board of Lev.

A board of you

One of the best pieces of advice received before I got underway as a CEO was from a highly regarded real estate fund management CEO. He suggested that I surround myself with people who have my best interests at heart but are not like-minded. The idea is that you form these people into the unofficial 'board of you'. Key to this 'personal board' is that the people you select are not from your family, social or business circles; their job is to act as your guides, provide you with a sounding board, help you to figure things out, give you honest, direct feedback and, if necessary, realign your moral compass. There will be times that you are in a world of pain and you will need constructive advice and criticism to support you in your role.

My personal board comprised a number of invaluable members. First, that CEO who suggested the idea in the first place agreed to offer ongoing support. He provided crucial business feedback and was vital in maximizing my professional capability, as well as providing alternative perspectives when it came to making decisions.

I've already introduced John Connolly. As consiglieri, John had an unerring ability to cut through the noise and reduce to absolute clarity communications, critical for a CEO. John Churchill, my lawyer, provided so much more than technical legal advice on contracts. A great lawyer can give you critical advice and look at the issues you are facing in a clear unemotional state. John Churchill provided me with options and a range of possible outcomes.

My best mates, who have been through thick and thin with me, are always available on the phone or for a coffee, to listen to the latest half-baked idea or total fuck up. Their counsel is always given with my best interests at heart and even though I might not like it, is always much appreciated.

Last, but certainly not least, I'd recommend a therapist or business coach. It took me a while to let down my guard and not to try to portray myself in the best possible light at all times. When I did open up completely, my therapist-coach was there to help me to learn from my mistakes, and create that resilience we talked about above. Too many CEOs burn out and often for reasons that can be avoided. A coach or therapist can offer preventative steps.

These professionals and friends have provided me with a fabulous safety net beneath the tightrope I walked daily as a CEO. I can't recommend a 'board of you' highly enough.

Ex-CEO and experienced non-executive director, Samantha Martin-Williams, is also passionate about the power of mentors, having benefitted as a mentee herself as well as acting as a mentor in organizations and board roles throughout her career. For Martin-Williams, it's all about 'partnership and purpose', with trust at the core of the relationship. That mentor relationship involves the acquisition of knowledge, insights, guidance or advice. And it's not always a comfortable experience: 'Over the years, I have been challenged by mentors, for example, to be more mindful, to develop self-management and self-awareness, to think about my impact on others.' However, these are precisely the kinds of things that drive personal and professional growth and resilience. As well as being invaluable sounding boards, good mentors provide these opportunities for growth.

Professional networks

As I suggested in Chapter 2, joining professional networks is crucial. These are the peers who are going to form your support base, your contacts list and your competitors as the pyramid narrows at the top of your careers. Young leaders will become top leaders in time, so join as soon as you start your career.

Industry associations

Industry associations can also provide a knowledge base critical for the learning you'll need to keep sharpening the tools of your trade and identify the trends that affect the community in which your business operates. For Tahnoon Pasha, having a significant body of knowledge about management in general will also help you when the going gets tough, when you reach what he calls your 'inflection point' and feel tempted to fall back on familiar old skills and experience rather than press ahead as CEO.

It might sound trite, but joining industry associations also allows you to give something back to your profession. Don't sit back, moaning about the impact of government policy and regulation on your business. Get active, lobby and provide that government with well-researched alternatives; you really can make a difference.

The value of industry associations

The legendary ex-CEO of the Property Council of Australia (PCA) and Asia Pacific Real Estate Association (APREA), Peter Verwer, has some interesting views about the value of industry associations. According to Verwer, the most successful of them:

- Knit together a community of interests.

- Help members make markets by growing their networks and broadening their horizons.

- Nurture professionalism by setting standards of performance, upskilling and celebrating excellence.

- Foster informed, transparent and trusted marketplaces.

- Provide a respected voice of leadership.

- Advocate the interests of its members while respecting an industry's responsibilities to society more widely.

- Shape public policy platforms, set industry standards and share ideas about market trends and giving back to your industry.

- Offer the camaraderie and fun of socializing with friends and peers (and rivals).

Last, but not least, in the words of Verwer himself: 'Perhaps the greatest benefit of industry association membership is the opportunity to help your industry define its own destiny.'

Your family and friends

Work–life balance is a tricky concept, even at the best of times. It may be true that, when it comes to being CEO, there is no such thing as balance; only trade-offs.

Preparing your family for life with a CEO in the house, or more to the point *not* in the house, is without doubt one of the hardest tasks in readiness for the CEO role. Remember that reaching this apex in a company may have been your work life ambition, but it is undoubtedly not theirs. You need their love and support and you might not get it if you are a knucklehead. The biggest problem can be absenteeism, evident even when you are actually sitting with the family at the kitchen table. Your mind will be elsewhere. But remember that your family is invaluable when it comes to switching off, to immersing yourself in something other than work – and, if you let them, they'll also keep you grounded.

I recall sitting down my sons, Jack and Sam, and telling them that, instead of completing my role and returning to live with them in Sydney, as planned, I was about to undertake a new job that would keep me in Singapore. But, I protested, it was only for three years and there would be a 'pot of gold' at the end of it. Jack, ever the adult in our relationship, looked me square in the eyes. 'I will be 14 by then,' he protested, and then lanced me with 'it had better be a big pot!'

As with all of the things we've covered in this chapter, you'll need to be intentional about making time for the people who mean the most to you.

As a CEO, it is your duty to look after yourself, so that you can be the strong leader that the organization needs. Understand that you need downtime. Accept that you are not an island. You'll be able to take better decisions and have more clarity and purpose if you take time away from the day job and connect with *all* stakeholders from your shareholders and staff through to family and friends.

Being a good CEO is essentially a trade-off between humility and omnipotence; you have to have a measure of both to undertake a role of this importance and complexity. But in the end, humility should win over. It is essential that, as a CEO, you stay humble, assess decisions in light of new information or changing circumstances, and surround yourself with honest and forthright people who will keep your hubris in check. Recognize that the title does not immediately bestow the right to give orders or automatic loyalty. Like all good leaders, the CEO needs to perpetually earn the respect of their organization and its stakeholders.

The respondents in the Egon Zehnder survey we looked at in Chapter 2 were often candid when it came to communicating their coping strategies for maintaining their energy.[2] One went on record as saying that: 'Maintaining personal energy and the sense of wellbeing has been the most surprising and difficult part of the role.' He found his answer in two ways: first, creating time in his calendar every day to just think and prioritize to maximize his personal impact, and, second, by creating time during his weekend to participate in an activity that took his mind off work.

Whatever the pressures, you cannot let the role of CEO become all-encompassing. The ability to reflect, maintain balance and stay grounded will serve you well, and help you to the rewarding, successful, meaningful CEO career you deserve.

If you let the role define you, you are well on your way to guaranteeing your ultimate demise as a CEO and the debilitating relevance deprivation we will deal with later in the book. You need to stay detached from the role, keeping your true persona separate, but maintaining focus to ensure that you are the best CEO you can be without that becoming all-consuming. It's a difficult but necessary balance.

---

[2] Egon Zehnder, *The CEO: A personal reflection*, 2018. Available from www.egonzehnder.com/CEO-study-2018 [accessed 18 August 2020].

4

A Job in Your Sights

'I thought I had it figured out. Man, was I wrong. I had no idea what I was in for.'

CEO, McKinsey CEO-elect survey, 2005[1]

PICTURE THE SCENE. I'd just landed the CEO job of my dreams. I'm feeling pretty good about myself. It's Day 1, and I've called a staff meeting to introduce myself and to plant some flags around vision and expectations. I was probably anticipating a degree of hushed reverence, at least the chance to be heard. What I got instead was a wall of resentment. It soon became clear that I had some unexpected challenges to face, not least the fact that a fair chunk of my people had not had a pay rise for several years.

It was not a great start, and it left me feeling blindsided almost before I'd begun. You couldn't have known, you might say. But the hard truth is that I probably could have found out if I'd dug deep enough and asked more about morale when doing my due diligence before taking on the role.

Most of us look at a new job at a new company like we look at a new romance. Both of you are on your best behaviour. Both of

---

[1] K. P. Coyne and B. S. Y. Rao, 'A guide for the CEO-elect', McKinsey & Company, 1 August 2005. Available from www.mckinsey.com/featured-insights/leadership/a-guide-for-the-ceo-elect [accessed 18 August 2020].

you only look for the good things in the other. Both of you run the risk of rushing in too early to make a commitment. Both of you will consciously keep secrets or withhold information that's important.

But beware. If due diligence is important when considering *any* role, it assumes an even greater importance when it comes to going for the top job. As well as getting your own house in order – reflecting and working on that resilience we talked about in Chapter 3 – you need to turn detective and find out as much as you can about the company you may be joining.

Forewarned is forearmed: Due diligence

Chronologically, due diligence should come before you put yourself in the race for the job and well before the contract stage. Apart from anything else, due diligence is a crucial part of your armoury in the interview process; knowledge is gold. You can get a great sense of the company by asking the right questions and, more importantly, listening to the responses; did they answer your questions appropriately, or at all?

As I found out to my cost, extensive due diligence is also vital if and when you do get the job. You don't have to be an expert, but you do have to know enough to be confident you can ask the right questions and also give considered answers to the questions that will be fired at you. And, when in post, remember that your initial interaction, often based on what you've learnt before you join – whether you show willingness to listen and learn, the way you ask questions and how you approach team members – will set the tone for your tenure.

Here are some things to consider.

Look beneath the surface

Consider the company website as a guide only, offering just the public face. You need to know what lies beneath that shiny skin.

Gather as much information as you can, from all sources. Google the company, the board members, the executives, the shareholders, the investors, the customers and suppliers. Check the gossip columns and the analysts' report. Talk to associates in the industry. Ask the headhunters who put you forward for the role to let you know how many CVs they received for the position – this will give you an indication of the market's perception of the company.

Find out why the last CEO left/is leaving

Are they now in the courts? In jail? It is a good sign if they have moved on to a better job. If they are 'taking a break to spend more time with their family' or 'looking for new opportunities', you are in trouble. At interview time, ask the Chair and the board about the past CEO, what their chief concerns are and what are their top priorities for a new CEO.

Be a strategic pessimist

It is better to expect that the company is in worse shape than anyone in the organization will let on. Remember: you will be held responsible for the performance of the company from Day 1, so you owe it to yourself to get to know as much as you can in advance.

Be sure you have enough information about the company's financial position. If you're looking at a turnaround situation, make sure there is enough money in the bank to pay for any redundancies or severance packages.

Interrogate key relationships

What are relations between teams like? Does finance regard marketing as a bunch of expensive dilettantes and junior staff regard seniors as lazy and ineffectual? See if you can spend more informal time with staff to find out.

Make your mind up about the Chair and the board

Your relationship with the organization's Chair will be crucial. Has he or she recently been a CEO and this is their first time at the top of the board? The Chair is your boss and the relationship will either make or break your career. Be pragmatic. The best you can hope for is a Chair who has your back... until they don't!

Make sure the wider board understands the balance between challenge, support and interference. Ask to see some sets of recent board papers to assess what the recurring issues are and how quickly they are resolved.

Learn the politics or who is literally and metaphorically sleeping with whom

Every company has its own tribes, its own dirty little secrets and, more importantly, little groups who owe someone for looking after them. Most people meet their partners, lifetime or romantic, at work. It's important to know how the top team works on a human level.

What does the market think?

Particularly for public companies, small shareholders are nice and, occasionally, you'll need them, but the ones that will make or break you are the top 20 or 30, the proxy advisors and the corporate governance 'experts'. Talk to analysts and investors once it's been announced you're taking over. Get the real story on the company and the board and continue to suck up information from various sources from then on.

What do your competitors think?

Talk to your competitors; regard them as peers. They'll be keen to meet you because they'll want to see the style of person that has taken over their competitor and what that's likely to mean to them.

Get the right deal – the contract

Congratulations! You've just been offered the job. You're on your way to becoming the CEO you've dreamed of becoming. Enjoy the moment. But don't let the euphoria get in the way of making sure the deal is right. Get a lawyer. Even if you think you know your way around an employment contract, you need someone with specialist knowledge to assure you that your new employers have your best interests at heart and feel confident that nothing will go wrong under your watch. And, without wishing to dampen spirits too much, you need to strike the best financial deal you can muster because, as strange as it sounds, your next role after being a CEO is likely to be even harder to get. The statistics say you may be 'between jobs' for, at best, 12 months.

Lawyer and 'Board of Lev' member John Churchill has seen more than his fair share of senior appointment contracts and has invaluable advice on unpacking them if things go pear-shaped after the handshaking stops. According to John, 'It is a complex area. My approach, before we open the contract, is to start a strategic discussion with my client, the potential CEO. Just because you've been offered the job doesn't mean you have to accept it.'

His experience also leads him to believe that many first-time CEOs will rush in and accept the job in their overwhelming enthusiasm to get their first gig (as I did!). This is not a great start and increases the chances that things might end badly. John also uses the analogy of love and romance: you may be all starry-eyed at the outset, but you could end up fighting over who gets the cat and the dog. Better to be hard-nosed and realistic about the details of the deal, work out your negotiating strategy and your walk-away position; then you can focus on getting the fundamentals right.

Whatever other details may be important to you individually, always focus on the following:

What is your role?

This may sound obvious, but the contract needs to state, in very clear language, the details of your actual position. For example, there is a distinction between a Chief Executive Officer alone, or a CEO combined with a Managing Director; they mean different things and have different powers and responsibilities. The reporting lines have to be very clear. Make sure you have the right to hire and fire as you see fit.

Companies can offer a standard contract for every employee. Don't accept obvious boilerplate around working hours, or anything that suggests that 'you may be employed to do this job but you will do whatever job your skills allow you to do while you are working for us and we can transfer you as we see fit.' Make sure they can't unilaterally send you off to do something that is completely different from your primary role, as that is the one on which you will ultimately be judged.

What will you be paid?

The money component of the contract has to be extremely clear. There is usually clarity around the base salary, but any Long-Term Incentive Plan (LTIP) components can be complicated and leave you with little room for negotiation. Interrogate the basis on which any incentives will be based; share price is to be avoided, as it's not great to have your remuneration based on something over which you ultimately have little or no control. According to Alex Edmans, Professor of Finance at the London Business School, referencing *The Purposeful Company's Study on Deferred Shares* (2019),[2] share price movements are a proxy for good management if measured over a long time such as 10 years, but the typical three-year timeframe is not enough. LTIPs are often applied to earnings before interest, taxes, depreciation and amortization (EBITDA), which is more appropriate, but whatever the metric, they are often not entirely within your control. Proceed with caution.

How can they get rid of you?

This is an area that needs to be better understood. In the past, CEO contracts were for a five-year period, but don't be misled: according to John Churchill, 'your contract only lasts as long as your notice period, generally around six months.' Shareholders and others often lament that CEOs are financially overrewarded. But, conceptually, the CEO role is like a high-wire act and it is easy to get blown off the wire. When push comes to shove, you probably have fewer rights than people on the shop floor and, for some roles, the likelihood of you getting another job any time soon is remote. John describes CEO pay as 'danger money'; many CEOs won't work, or work at that level, again, whether they have put in a good or a bad performance.

How can you leave?

The six-month notice period also works for the CEO too. But Churchill advises CEOs never to resign, even if the job has become unbearable, as this gives you zero negotiating power. As soon as you say you want to resign, clause x in your contract kicks in. You'll get six months' notice, will be put on gardening leave, classified as a bad leaver and you won't get any of your benefits

---

[2] The Purposeful Company, *The Purposeful Company study on deferred shares: Key findings report*, 2019. Available from www.biginnovationcentre-purposeful-company.com/wp-content/uploads/2019/10/tpc-deferred-shares-study-key-findings-report-final-web-version.pdf [accessed 18 August 2020].

and bonuses. In his experience, there's generally a deal to be done. Either a company will have to sack you or you come to a mutual agreement. Once again, the devil is in the detail. Get a lawyer on board to help you.

However you leave, and under whatever circumstances, a contentious, public separation is never a good thing: it can severely affect your ability to find your next job, put any accumulated stock options at risk (depending on your successor) and could affect your reputation forever. Some would-be CEOs ask for an outline plan or agreement, between the board and themselves, which details how any separation process will look. It doesn't form part of the contract itself, but can be an invaluable guide if things don't go as planned. And, as we'll discover in later chapters, board succession should be a regular part of board discussions; it's good practice for the company and for you.

The CEO-elect

Back in 2005, management consultants McKinsey interviewed some top CEOs,[3] a mix of external and internal hires, about how newly designated CEOs can improve their chances of success in the vital period between taking the job and arriving in post. Those in the know – who understood that it's just not possible to turn up as an all-conquering hero – believed that there's a great deal that a newly designated CEO can accomplish before turning up on Day 1. Continuing the process of due diligence before they arrived meant getting a head start when diagnosing and addressing their own shortcomings and in understanding the organization and its

---

[3] K. P. Coyne and B. S. Y. Rao, 'A guide for the CEO-elect', McKinsey & Company, 1 August 2005. Available from www.mckinsey.com/featured-insights/leadership/a-guide-for-the-ceo-elect [accessed 18 August 2020].

other leaders better, as well as identifying resources needed to smooth the transition.

For McKinsey, this boiled down into some key factors:

Seize the day

Surveyed CEOs reinforced that getting insights into how the company is perceived, its weaknesses and strengths, *before* their appointment was announced was invaluable. Newly designated CEOs have more control over their time before the announcement. Once the world learns the news, the demands from stakeholders and the media start to build up. Don't be tempted to use all of the time to tie up loose ends in your current role; think ahead too.

Identify and attack areas of weakness

CEOs also used this crucial period to continue the process of personal reflection and assessment, tackling any weaknesses they may have in relation to the specific role they'd be taking on. This could take the form of external training, meeting with industry peers, coaching or spending time with the old CEO.

Get to know the board

Get to know each board member on a personal level as early as possible. The surveyed CEOs emphasized the importance of getting to know each board member individually, identifying any board factions and continuing to tease out their expectations for you.

Have a story ready before Day 1

While it's not unreasonable to give a new CEO time to develop a more detailed strategy, your more immediate pronouncements will still be pored over and scrutinized. Have a story ready. Projecting confidence without making baseless promises may be hard, but you'll need to formulate some sort of statement for stakeholders.

Get help for unpleasant tasks
This is not always possible, but outgoing CEOs can be a valuable resource when it comes to clearing the decks and making unpalatable policy or employee decisions ahead of your arrival. If you can collaborate like this, it will bring about the changes you know are needed but protect you from immediate fall-out when you arrive.

Find a confidant
You'll need someone to talk to, that trusted sounding board and advisor we've already talked about in Chapter 3. This was an essential for the CEOs surveyed by McKinsey.

Beware civic duties
As soon as their new positions were announced, CEOs in the survey found themselves overwhelmed with requests from all sorts of organizations and causes. Be cautious about accepting the first or too many requests. Postponing any decisions on this kind of involvement is recommended.

Many of you will already have been involved with merger and acquisition activity. You wouldn't dream of doing a deal without proper due diligence and a robustly negotiated contract. You need to take the same approach when it comes to your own 'mergers'. Think, too, about how you can spend the time continuing and extending your due diligence between getting the job and Day 1. Forewarned really is forearmed.

Part 2

Peak #1: The first 100 days

5

Preparing the Ground: The First 100 Days

'Give me six hours to chop down a tree and I will spend the first four sharpening the axe.'

Abraham Lincoln

'CONGRATULATIONS ON YOUR appointment. So what will you do differently?' asked John Connolly before my first CEO gig. I was ready for his question. I had decided that I would move my desk from my predecessor's isolated office to the main open-plan area. Connolly thought it a great idea. I thought it would really help me to get to know the company and my colleagues, to show how accessible I wanted to be. Unfortunately, we were on our own: cue a whole host of objections from HR, facilities and compliance concerned about status, confidentiality and – more simply – space. 'Humour me,' I said. But when I arrived on my first day, the desk had been encircled with so many palms and plants that it looked like I was to be stationed in a jungle clearing. Despite my best intentions, no one wanted the boss sitting right next to them. I was in danger of disrespecting cultural and hierarchical norms; it was a change too far, too soon.

Think back to a time you were told there was a new boss coming. Chances are it made you a bit nervous. You definitely googled him or her. You talked about what the new boss might be like with colleagues and friends. What would he or she do first? Who would he or she keep and who would go?

Whether you've been promoted from within or you're new to the organization, the announcement that you've got the job will trigger this kind of reaction in the company, and it'll be happening at all levels. It's a natural reaction to change.

The good and bad news is that your people will attach a lot of meaning to what you say and, more importantly, what you do, for the first two or three months. Everything you do will communicate something. At the same time, you'll be in a honeymoon period with these same people, your board, investors and the media. You'll never have a better chance to communicate your values and your priorities, to make the changes you need or to set in train a quick turnaround. The longer you wait, the harder it'll be. But it's also not a time for knee-jerk reactions and plans that are ill-thought-through and not properly tested.

When I was preparing for my first CEO role, my mentor John Connolly gave me some invaluable advice about my first 100 days. John understands that CEOs are often judged on their initial performance – perceptions that can be hard to shift if things don't go as planned. For him, the three key areas where a new CEO can fail are:

- not forging effective relationships with those who can impact the personal and company success;
- not setting realistic expectations that address key issues and failing to deliver on those expectations;
- not demonstrating a personal understanding of the job and the organization.

Your first 100 days, then, is a period both of opportunities and dangers. It's the first peak you'll need to scale in your time as CEO. You may be feeling pressure to justify your appointment or get some quick results. If you've been promoted internally, you may have some biases about you to overcome; if you've come from the outside, a lack of baggage will be balanced by the need to get up to speed with the organization and its culture. All the time, you'll be getting used to unprecedented levels of scrutiny. While the specifics of the CEO role and experience will be different just about everywhere, I believe that there are three immutable truths consistent with any new appointment:

1. Every CEO starts the new job with enthusiasm, drive and energy.
2. Senior management teams can make or break a CEO's tenure.
3. You have never been more on your own in a workplace.

That's what I discovered when I tackled my own first 100 days. The jungle encampment was just the start.

The first 100 days: Why and what

The idea of a first 100-days leadership benchmark comes from the world of politics, especially in relation to US Presidents. Pundits and press will pore over every pronouncement for early signs of performance and trends that give an impression of what might be to come; what kind of leader that person might be. It's the same for new CEOs.

It can be a difficult balancing act, combining the need to appraise the company as part of longer-term planning while also dealing with the most immediate concerns. However much due diligence you've done, there is always more to find out, questions you didn't or couldn't ask in advance, or that were only half-answered, answered evasively or downright untruthfully. 'Are we solvent?' is a great question; 'It depends' the worst possible answer.

Getting to know, and working with, your board and senior management team will be crucial to your investigations in those early days. You can't know everything, and you'll need to take them along with you to work out necessary changes. Rash decisions are not the order of the early days; do not walk in and fire someone. Do not respond 'off the bat' to any questioning; be open about the need to do further research. All stakeholders will assume that you will want to meet with them face to face. This can be both a trap and a waste of time; be selective.

The view from the top

I asked John Poynton, a highly experienced Australian director, what he wished he had been told when taking on his first CEO role.

The first thing he identified was the critical importance of a CEO's relationship with the Chair and the board. He also advocates listening – a lot – working on your EQ. Have a medium-term outlook and don't allow yourself to be whipsawed by 'short termism', as that will colour your thinking and distract you from the focus you need on the longer-term viability of your company: as CEO, it's up to you to steer it to a sustainable future.

More than anything, back yourself: you have been appointed because you are deemed to have the requisite experience and qualifications. Never forget that.

Your 100-day plan sets the tone for the rest of your appointment. You need to present yourself, internally and externally, as balanced, fair and appropriately qualified and experienced for the job. Spend your time listening rather than issuing proclamations. Develop a filter to make sense of the advice with which you'll be inundated. Get buy-in from senior management and trusted external consultants, so that issues can be quickly identified, prioritized and acted on, while making plans for the company's strategy for growth.

Gather knowledge about the company, the market, the roles people play. Get to know your assets and products, both by industry reading and discussion with senior management. Walk the assets, the products or the floors of your operations. Go out with frontline salespeople. Meet some key customers. Talk to your people; it might sound trite but they are your assets too. Gauge their reaction to you.

This is also the time to question everything; do not accept 'But it's always been done this way.' When I started my first CEO role, I assumed all the heads of department knew what they were doing and were aligned with the company's direction and values. As soon as I started questioning them on their business knowledge and skill set, it became clear that some of them simply didn't have the capability to do their jobs, or lacked the intellectual curiosity to look for better ways to do things. That was a situation I had to address. I needed people firing on all cylinders who could learn from unexpected events or mistakes. Keep asking questions. Later on, this might seem like micro-managing; right now, it's an acceptable part of your fact-finding mission.

Remember, too, that even the best-laid 100-day plan is unlikely to survive contact with the enemy. It will need to be regularly and significantly reworked, based on what you find out and unforeseen events. For example, if the staff have been poorly managed and morale is low, with people on the verge of leaving (as I found to my cost first time out), you will definitely need to rejig things, take those specific circumstances into account and make sure that the foundations of the platform are firm before adding the additional stresses of a new business strategy.

Above all, there are some things you'll just need to accept:

You haven't done enough due diligence

No matter how much information you were given or have found out, and even if you've been promoted internally, you are still an outsider. Don't get discouraged. Realize there is much more that you need to know than you originally thought, and plan accordingly.

You are now in the spotlight

You'll be expected to answer questions about things like staffing and strategy, about assets or products that you simply can't yet answer. Give yourself a cushion. Respect the question, but don't try to answer it unless you have sufficient confidence in your existing level of knowledge to give an appropriate response. You have one chance to make a good first impression; don't blow it.

You won't have all the information you need

You'll be asked to take decisions without having all the information, so don't fall into the trap of taking actions prematurely simply to show people how clever you are. In Chapter 9, we'll be discussing Colin Powell's maxim on making decisions based on his 40/70 principle. For now, suffice it to say that you will never have all the information required to make a perfect decision, but a mix of enough information, instinct based on years of experience and a genuine desire to do the right thing is much better than 'paralysis by analysis'.

You need to be flexible

This will be a steep learning curve. Be pragmatic and adapt your approach as circumstances dictate. But don't flex so much that you allow yourself to be whipsawed by competing interests and suggestions.

The questions you ask will not be fully answered

You won't be the only one on their best behaviour. People will naturally want to show themselves in the best possible light. You'll encounter obfuscation and half-truths. Take note of the way any question is answered as much as the answer itself: is the responder wary? Do they have the information readily to hand? Are they confident? Are they accepting responsibility or palming it off on someone else?

You need to build trust – fast

Trust is the glue that holds organizations together. It's critical that you build trust quickly, but it's also one of the hardest things to do. The board needs to trust that you are equal to the role. Your senior executives need to trust that you will not 'throw them under a bus' at the first sign of trouble. Investors and other stakeholders will be keenly watching your performance in the early days to assess whether you are someone they can do business with, and whether you are a safe pair of hands at the wheel of the organization.

You need your senior management team to be on board...

Engage and converse with senior management in a respectful, open manner. Assess their perceptions of you. Ask them about their career aspirations. Help them to be a loyal team member. Acknowledge that they were loyal to your predecessor and you may be an unwanted intruder. Reinforce your expectations of them in terms of respect, empathy, integrity and trust and, unless you have reasons otherwise, indicate you are looking forward to a long, harmonious working relationship.

...but that's not always possible. Backstabbing is a fact

Backstabbing will exist, because people want your job. Recognize and deal with that fact or you'll be off to a bad start. In the minds of some of your senior management team, maybe a displaced interim CEO, the way to the top is through the person currently in the role. You will continue to be undermined until you deal with it. Ultimately, disloyalty can't be allowed to continue and honest conversations will have to be had: 'As part of my team, I would die in a ditch for you and all I expect in return is your loyalty. If you aren't happy, I will help you find another job, but the backstabbing stops now.' If it doesn't, changes will need to be made with speed and efficiency, both to restore morale and check the behaviour of others who may be watching how you deal with unacceptable situations.

Your days are numbered, statistically

You know the statistics around the average length of CEO tenure. The clock is already ticking. Don't fight and rail against the harsh reality; instead, position yourself to meet the requirements and challenges of your next job, while being present in your current one.

Master the transition

Writing in the *Harvard Business Review*,[1] Michael D. Watkins believes that we tend to focus on the first 100 days phenomenon not because we expect our leaders to come out of the other side with a long list of achievements, but because the early days in the job mark an important transition. These transitions represent some of the most challenging times for leaders and, not unreasonably, how a leader negotiates their transition period is often seen as a significant indicator for what happens next.

Transitions are times when momentum builds or it doesn't, when opinions about the new leader begin to crystallize, when early wins can build credibility and capital. Significant missteps might be hard to reverse. In the words of Watkins:

> The first hundred days mark is not the end of the story, it's the end of the beginning. Leaders entering new roles

---

[1] M. D. Watkins, 'Why the first 100 days matters', *Harvard Business Review*, 23 March 2009. Available from https://hbr.org/2009/03/why-the-first-100-days-matters [accessed 18 August 2020].

can stumble badly and still recover. But it's a whole lot easier if they don't stumble in the first place. And that's why the transition period matters so much.

A Bates Communications report on a CEO's first 100 days[2] includes a useful series of *Eight Must-Avoid Traps for New Senior Leaders*. The report acknowledges the tension between wanting and needing quick results and biding your time while you get your feet under the table. It's a good guide to the pitfalls that might cause some of that first 100 days stumbling:

1. Overemphasizing quick decisions and action
2. Trying to prove that you're smarter than everyone on the team
3. Not focusing on building relationships with important audiences
4. Underestimating people's need to know you
5. Lack of deliberate choices about communication vehicles/styles
6. Overlooking the importance of setting and managing expectations
7. Losing control of your calendar
8. Failing to think about how you want to be remembered after your last 100 days

We'll be returning to a number of these themes in future chapters. For now, make sure you avoid your own jungle encampment moment.

---

[2] S. Weighart, *Your first 100 days as CEO: Eight must-avoid traps*, Bates Communications. Available from www.bates-communications.com/hs-fs/hub/25382/file-13529443-pdf/docs/guide_to_the_first_100_days._bates_communications.pdf [accessed 18 August 2020].

6

Introducing the CEO playbook: A blueprint for success

'The only impossible journey is the one you never begin.'

Tony Robbins

CLIMBING MOUNTAINS CAN be a tricky business. And it's not only mountaineers who are psychologically drained by false peaks, steep rises and rough terrain. CEOs also have to develop the mental toughness to take what's thrown at them. As you approach each day, you'll be battling inner and outer issues. There's the inner struggle of feeling well prepared and ready for your role as a CEO, alongside your inner fears – those temporary, disheartening feelings of being an imposter and not being up to the demands of the job at hand. Then there are the outer issues, those things you have little or no control over and which might have you soaring to the heights one day and plummeting headlong towards the depths the next.

This roller coaster of emotions will become part of your daily routine. Knowing how to deal with the obstacles you meet on the way – whether coming from internal fears or unexpected external blows – is a challenge not to be taken lightly. To achieve success as a CEO, you have to acknowledge that your tenure is not a sprint but a marathon. It requires sustained, arduous work to be the winner at the end of an intense term. As we've seen, the CEO tenure calls for intense preparation ahead of time and regular re-energizing along the way. It also means being armed with the best possible strategy, one that will not only empower the team but also motivate and enhance their productivity so that ultimately the company and key stakeholders end up winning too.

I've learnt the hard way that there are some significant steps you can take to sustain you for the journey. That's why I've developed my own *CEO playbook*, which has enabled me to take, manage and sell one company, and guide another through a horribly complex IPO.

My blueprint comprises four steps:

1. Take control
2. Set the culture
3. Take responsibility for the direction of the company
4. Run the business

Take control

On my first day as a CEO, I called everybody to a town hall meeting and told them that I was there to support them, to assist them to achieve their potential, to trust them to do the jobs entrusted to them, and to help them to develop themselves, achieve an optimal work/life balance, enjoy coming to work, and be rewarded commensurate with effort. A sea of blank faces stared back at me and I realized that I had not done what I had first been taught in the Navy – take charge.

One of the first things you are taught on the Navy's New Entry Officers' Course is just that: to 'Take Control'. As a CEO, you need to take the right approach and assume leadership from the very beginning. You can only really set the company's direction once you have assumed command of the company in the first place and are trusted by your teams to lead it.

On that same course, we were lectured on leadership by the base Executive Officer (XO). She was a tough, uncompromising ex-nurse, universally feared for her rigid, disciplinarian approach. As a team, my fellow recruits and I were keen just to get through her lecture and then get on with the fun stuff of learning 'how to drive ships and blow shit up'. But she took command of the room in an instant, sizing us all up perfectly. 'I know that none of you here like me, no one here does and I don't give a fuck!' was her opening gambit. She certainly had our attention. 'I am not here to be liked; I am here to ensure that the captain's orders are carried out and that you head into the fleet as officers, ready to lead. Be authentic and be consistent, don't play favourites and don't try to be liked; you will look weak and no one follows weak leaders.' I would have done well to have remembered that exhortation in the years that followed.

I squandered some of my first 100 days' goodwill by failing to recognize that I was not there to give people what they wanted, but to ensure the organization got what it needed. My well-meaning attempt at soft encouragement just didn't work. I was there to maximize the company's potential and give employees a safe platform within which to work. The organization I was taking on was not the same as the one I had left. I needed to take a different approach.

Take charge and tell your team you are there to lead them. You are taking responsibility for all aspects of the business: the decisions, strategies, opportunities and issues right from the first day of your appointment. That doesn't mean you'll be doing it alone; you'll need to work hard to create a team that will feel aligned with your goals and committed to implementing them. But once you've made it clear that you're taking charge, they'll know they are accountable to someone – and that you'll have their backs by generating success from which they can all benefit. Although you will trust them to do their work effectively, that work will be subject to review, so they need to be responsible, productive and accountable.

Set the culture

The tone really does come from the top. Don't walk in with the demeanour of an all-conquering emperor, impervious to the fears and concerns of your team. Arrive early, watch the floor fill, note the interactions, feel the sense of uncertainty that accompanies change; be humble.

Recognize that your demeanour – whether it is happy, sad or angry – will be reflected in the demeanour of the whole organization. It's what psychologists call 'emotional contagion', and it can be particularly potent in leaders. If you show agitation, agitation will spread. If you are positive, you'll create a much more conducive environment for getting great results. Consistency also matters. I realized that my mood set the tone for the organization. Every time I acted in a different way or was involved in projects in different ways, the teams became confused and concerned, because I wasn't giving them clear and consistent signals.

As the CEO, you dictate the spirit of the organization. If I walked onto the floor in a bad mood, the whole morale of the company went down. I didn't anticipate how much of an impact my mood had on the overall organization. I learnt the crucial lesson that self-awareness and self-control – two key elements of Goleman's emotional intelligence – can have a huge impact on tone and culture.

Setting the right culture also means walking the talk when it comes to values, to doing the right thing. Regardless of circumstances, you want your company to be made up of good corporate citizens who respect the rights and needs of all citizens. Commit to doing the right thing.

Take responsibility for the direction of the company

Once you're past your first 100 days, it's time for some serious planning. It's important to have clarity of purpose, to communicate it clearly and to motivate everyone in the organization – either directly or through trusted sponsors – to get on board for the journey.

Taking responsibility for the direction of the company is about developing and executing a strategic plan. Getting strategy right is a fundamental and essential task for CEOs and the organizations they run. It means building on your early work on vision and culture, assessing where the company is now, its market position and potential, and then setting out strategic choices for the company you want to be and how to get there.

Strategy has to be dynamic, able to adapt and evolve as your company and the environment in which it operates changes. You need to be able to measure its success as it unfolds and adjust as necessary. Most of all, it needs to be communicated effectively, both inside and outside the company. Effective strategy is clear and makes sense for all of the people responsible for making it happen.

Run the business

You also have to run the business, to be its leader. In the first place, this means managing yourself, showing the self-awareness and self-control you'll need to take full command. You'll also need to find a good routine for yourself, and to master the art of managing and protecting the limited time available to you, to prioritize and delegate. This is also a time for self-care, giving yourself the time to rest, recuperate and reflect. As we've already seen in Chapter 3, you'll be a better leader for it.

Being CEO means that you're at the centre of a complex web of stakeholders, with all that implies in terms of competing priorities and demands. Having a culture where governance, risk and compliance (GRC) is embedded in your culture will help you to navigate what can be tricky waters. Your relationship with your board and investors will be critical, and you ignore at your peril the compliance requirements set out by law and regulation, whether that's sector specific or generic employment and health and safety rules.

You'll be a fortunate CEO not to encounter at some point a crisis in your business – perhaps a hostile takeover, a market collapse or even (as we now know) a global pandemic. Having the right crisis management and business continuity plans in place will help. As with so much in the CEO job description, anticipation, planning and effective execution are key.

Over the next two chapters, we'll be looking at the first two key elements from the *CEO playbook* that, ideally, you'll look to achieve in the first 100 days: getting the right team in place and setting the vision and culture for the journey ahead. Once we're past the first 100 days, and onto our second peak (Part 3), we'll also return in more detail to strategy, leadership and how best to run the business.

7

Building and Leading Teams

'Talent wins games, but teamwork and intelligence win championships.'

Michael Jordan

IN A PERFECT world, an incoming CEO, especially a less experienced one, would arrive to lead a senior management team dedicated to working for his or her benefit, with everyone working together seamlessly towards a shared purpose and goals. Unfortunately, the upper echelon of the average company is unlikely to be such a welcoming or accommodating place for their new boss.

I found this out when I arrived to replace a CFO who had been acting as interim CEO. He felt he was in line for the CEO role proper and was clearly unhappy not to be selected. It took me some time to realize that he was undermining me, with some success, even with the board. This was only going to end with one outcome, and I regret not following my gut instinct and sacking the individual earlier. When he did leave, I was able to make much more positive progress, to the extent a board member later admitted that he had been adversely influenced by the views of our ex-CFO.

It seems that I am not alone. According to data from the CEO Genome Project (see Chapter 1), the single most common mistake among first-time CEOs – apparently committed by some 60% of them – is not getting the right team in place quickly enough:

For CEOs choosing talent, the stakes are high and the misses obvious. The successful ones move decisively to upgrade talent. They set a high bar and focus on performance relevant to the role rather than personal comfort or loyalty—two criteria that often lead to bad calls.[1]

Lesson learnt.

Adriana Giotta has an interesting take on leading teams. A good CEO will listen to and trust the senior team, but also recognizes that the buck stops with him or herself. She uses the metaphor 'good enough parent' to describe a CEO who responds to needs, but not wants. The key is to understand what those needs are, to be skilful at knowing and seeing what's going on. A leader, like a parent, may fear that if they don't respond to wants, then that person will become belligerent and angry. But if, instead, the leader provides clear frameworks and boundaries, people will feel safe and contained.

Senior management teams today

It is a great temptation for a newly minted CEO, especially in times of stress, to focus on their area of previous expertise. For example, if you have come from a sales background, you will attempt to burrow into that area and look for problems to fix. But, as CEO, you'll be responsible for everything. You can't just depend on what you know best; you'll need to build a team of C-suite colleagues who can help you take the strain. And that C-suite will need to be as on top of their game as you are.

---

[1] E. L. Botelho, K. R. Powell, S. Kincaid and D. Wang, 'What sets successful CEOs apart', *Harvard Business Review*, May–June 2017. Available from https://hbr.org/2017/05/what-sets-successful-ceos-apart [accessed 18 August 2020].

Research from Harvard Business School and Heidrick & Struggles[2] has identified six key C-level roles which, increasingly, are filled by people who are not just there as technical specialists. These days, CFOs are expected to handle complex risk management strategies and processes; CIOs to create business models; chief human resource officers to design succession plans and a talent structure that provide a competitive edge.

Six key C-suite roles

- Chief information officer
- Chief marketing and sales officer
- Chief financial officer
- General counsel
- Chief supply-chain management officer
- Chief human resources officer

Like their CEOs, the skills that helped them climb to the top aren't enough on their own when they get there. As organizations and the markets in which they operate become more complex, more multifaceted and more global, senior managers are expected to support the CEO on business strategies and also to offer their own insights and contribute to key decisions.

This means that *all* jobs at senior management level have shifted towards a focus on business acumen and more *human* leadership skills: communication, collaboration, strategic thinking. Technical skills are merely a starting point, the bare minimum. The researchers give the example of a CEO counting on a CIO to contribute

---

[2] B. Groysberg, L. K. Kelly and B. MacDonald, 'The new path to the C-suite', *Harvard Business Review*, March 2011. Available from https://hbr.org/2011/03/the-new-path-to-the-c-suite [accessed 18 August 2020].

to discussions about market expansion and the implications and challenges for IT. The message is clear: as CEO, you need a senior team around you that can actively add value to the organization as a whole rather than just being functional specialists.

So, how do you go about getting the right people in the right place at the right time?

Creating your own team

To whatever extent possible, try to pick your own senior leadership team. To get the job done, you simply must have your own people around you, people you can trust and whose values align with yours and the organization you are jointly creating. Recognize that the senior management team you're inheriting was somebody else's pick. They might have been ideal for that person, but that's no guarantee they'll work well for and with you. Difficult as it might be, you will probably need to bring in trusted colleagues from a previous leadership role, recruit new blood and prune the existing senior management team.

Aligning values

When you are making changes in your team, you'll go through some pain but the biggest lesson I learnt was to identify the values–ability mismatch. Many CEOs fail to identify the particular type of employees that can take a company to the precipice because, despite their high training and skills, they have the wrong attitude and are not aligned with the company's goals, values or vision. Figure 4 shows the value matrix I used to discover which type of people would be suitable to work for my companies, or not.

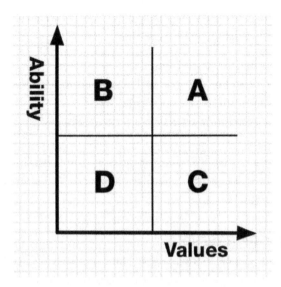

Figure 4: The values–ability matrix

Ideally, most of your team will have both high ability and share common values (employee type A). At the other end of the spectrum, it's easy to identify and get rid of those with low abilities and low values (type D). Type C employees who are on board with values but have low ability are not ideal either. The ones that are hardest to identify and make sense of are those with high ability and no alignment with the values of the company (type B).

Type Bs may talk the talk when it comes to company values, but they're not fully on board. When I first became a CEO, my type Bs were in danger of causing mayhem; they regularly created issues and simply took up too much management time. One of the most important lessons I learnt was to confront these outliers as soon as possible. By all means give them the opportunity to reassess their behaviours and actions, but they need to become true type As to stay the course for the long game.

Every CEO and organization will have their own values, but here are some I consider to be important:

- Doing the right thing
- The ability to listen and absorb contrarian views without taking them as a personal affront
- A general desire to ensure the wellbeing of others in the group
- A great desire to be a good corporate citizen
- The desire to be in alignment with the direction of the organization

The case for diversity

A team of values-aligned senior managers needn't imply a set of clones who all come from similar backgrounds and experiences or who all think in the same way. The case for demographic diversity at the highest level in organizations – whether in terms of gender, race, class or other characteristics – has been well made. McKinsey's 2018 *Delivering through Diversity* report[3] showed that more gender-diverse boards can improve performance by 21% while that figure rises to 35% for ethnically diverse boards. Recruiting for diversity might be seen as difficult in certain sectors, contexts or cultures, but it's increasingly a business must-have.

Diversity is not just a matter of demographics. Groupthink is a clear and present danger for senior teams. In his book, *Rebel Ideas*, Matthew Syed builds a compelling case for a more holistic view of diversity, using a wealth of examples to argue that the complex problems we face today require the collective intelligence offered by the power of *cognitive* diversity. If everyone in a team is like-

[3] McKinsey & Company, *Delivering through diversity*, January 2018. Available from www.mckinsey.com/~/media/mckinsey/business%20functions/organization/our%20insights/delivering%20through%20diversity/delivering-through-diversity_full-report.ashx [accessed 18 August 2020].

minded, then it's very easy to be blindsided by people outside the organization who might be benefitting from more 'outside-the-box' thinking. In HQ operational meetings in the Israeli army, they assign a 'devil's advocate', whose job it is to disagree with and pick holes in the operational plan, so that all aspects are covered. Make sure you have the people and the culture which enables and encourages robust debate and a range of viewpoints.

Remember, though, that once the debate has been concluded and agreement reached, collective responsibility then needs to kick in. Once you leave a meeting, everybody needs to put on a united front and, when the decision is communicated to the team, it must be owned by everyone.

Thinking ahead

You want to help people at all levels of the organization to develop and grow, so identify what the gaps are that are preventing people from taking the next role and put in place a plan to help them. The right kind of development can be a great motivator. Make sure all members of the team are given an allowance in time for them to pursue both professional and personal aspirations.

At the same time, make sure you have succession plans in place for all key roles. Identify the people you especially want to keep and those who are going to have a part in your own succession planning. You won't be there forever and you need to have the right people with the aptitude and appetite to step up. Start this succession planning within the first year: you could, after all, be hit by a bus.

Motivating your team

There's nothing quite like a talented, mutually supportive team motivated to strive for shared goals. Giving people the opportunity to develop themselves while doing their best work for you can create tremendous synergy and productivity.

Understand, too, that we're all individuals, likely to be motivated by different things, and sometimes different things act as motivators at different stages of our lives. Some things are short-term motivators, whereas the 'bounce' you get from others can be more long-lasting. Many people think that money is the greatest motivator, the only one that really matters, but that's a mistake. Sure, people need enough money to live their lives but, beyond that, and certainly for senior colleagues, other factors come into play.

Psychologist Frederick Herzberg had some interesting things to say about motivation at work. For Herzberg, job satisfaction and job dissatisfaction are not opposites: rather, the opposite of satisfaction is no satisfaction and the opposite of dissatisfaction is no dissatisfaction. Remedying the causes of dissatisfaction will not create satisfaction. It's a simple but effective way to think about what motivates people. The factors that lead to job satisfaction (like the ones outlined below) are completely separate from those that eliminate dissatisfaction, such as job security, a safe working environment and, yes, a fair wage.

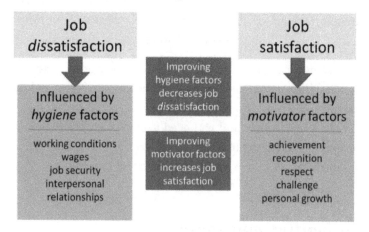

Figure 5: Herzberg's two factor theory of workplace motivation[4]

[4] F. Herzberg, B. Mausner and B. B. Snyderman, *The motivation to work*. Transaction Publishers, 1959.

If you want to motivate your team, you have to focus on positive, motivator factors like achievement, recognition and responsibility. People care about their role in where the organization is heading. They enjoy positive interactions with colleagues and the people they encounter daily, through their role. They are motivated by things like:

- opportunities for career advancement;
- opportunities for further education;
- personal development;
- being part of a winning team;
- the right financial incentives, linked to performance.

There's no one-size-fits-all. The money might have a short-term impact, but if other aspects of the job are unfulfilling, it won't last.

Every one of your people will have a different motivation or perspective for doing their particular job. One story to illustrate this is the three stonemasons story. There were three guys cutting stones. Somebody walks past and says: 'What are you doing?' The first stonemason replies: 'I'm banging rocks.' The second one says: 'I'm doing my job,' and the third one says: 'I'm building a cathedral.' Despite having the exact same job, these three stonemasons had three different perspectives. The person building the cathedral has a broader perception of what the job really entails and is able to see the big picture.

A team code of honour

I'm a big fan of team codes of honour, setting clear expectations about behaviour and culture. I would call my senior team together and say:

> Here is my code of honour. I expect you to be loyal. I'm prepared to die in a ditch for you. I'll always put your interests ahead of my own. I'll let you take the credit and

I'll shoulder the responsibility. All I ask in return is loyalty, to me, to the team and to the company. If you are disloyal, then you can expect to find employment elsewhere.

I expect you to look out for each other. If you try and score points by undermining or backstabbing each other, there are other organizations you can go to. I expect you to be culturally and emotionally aware. I expect you to behave properly at all times. You set the tone for the organization. Don't mess it up.

Codes of honour are mantras that need to be incorporated into your company's culture so that everyone has a clear vision. Everyone signs up, and it isn't subject to change, even in the toughest times. The code keeps everyone together, so you can all be successful.

Here are some key principles which underpin my code:

Nobody gets left behind

On the first day of Navy Initial Officer Training, we were instructed to assemble at 5.30 a.m. in full kit, ready for the day ahead. At the allotted time, there were four of us ready to go at the muster point, neatly turned out, uniforms ironed, shoes buffed, feeling very pleased with ourselves.

The Chief Petty Officer faced us and asked: 'What the fuck are you doing here?'

'Reporting as instructed,' we barked in unison.

'Where are your shipmates?' he barked and added: 'You've made yourselves look good but you've left your shipmates behind. What's the point of turning up to the battle without your full team? Go back and help them get ready!'

That was a very strong lesson learnt: look after each other. Nobody gets left behind. As an officer, you are expected to take charge and get done what you are required to do. But you need to bring people along with you. Look to identify what people need, not what they want. The vast majority of people at work want to do a good job, to develop and grow. Your job is to facilitate and encourage that, and make sure they get the support they need. Don't leave them behind.

Be consistent

We've already looked in Chapter 6 at how leaders have the power to influence the mood of the organization, for good and ill. A well as consistency of mood, you need to be consistent and even-handed when it comes to leadership. Don't pick favourites. Treat everyone the same with a consistent approach. Don't pander to people kissing your ass and don't support tribalism.

Live your mission

You have to walk the walk. Over the years, I've seen both good and bad leadership. The obvious difference is between those leaders who set a series of values and live by them, and those who spend months creating a series of mission statements and then debase them by doing the opposite. You've got to live your values and mission.

Leaders eat last

Make sure your team is fed and rested before you are. As the leaders of the company, the senior team has to make sure the whole team has the energy, resources and tools to accomplish the job at hand. Like you, they need to rest and recharge. They need opportunities for learning and development. They need the right support to have a great place to work and achieve their goals.

At social functions, I made sure I was the last person in the line to eat. It used to drive me mad when other senior leaders were the first to step to the head of the queue. A small thing, but an important example of setting the right tone, of doing the right thing.

Encourage competitive tension

You need to encourage competitive tension to strive and perform optimally. I'm not suggesting dog-eat-dog alpha cultures that do nothing other than create discord and tension, tribes and factions. But a little healthy competition maximizes productivity and, for some, is a strong motivating factor. Think carefully about how you achieve this though, and make sure you're not inadvertently leaving the less competitive-minded behind.

Be tough, but be kind

Don't allow yourself to be swayed by hard-luck stories and circumstances, but make sure you empathize and, where necessary, carry out random acts of kindness. Don't advertise it, but ensure you do it regularly. For example, if you have a senior colleague who has been working flat out on a project, give them some extra days off or the opportunity to work from home.

The bottom line for me when it comes to building and motivating teams is to be humble while still in command. Remember Adriana Giotta's thinking about leading teams: you are there to provide the frameworks and boundaries that enable others to do their work and find satisfaction in it. Some more words of wisdom from Rear Admiral Lee Goddard also reinforce this point. He has a mantra that *results are achieved with and through people, never at the expense of people.* The best CEOs are true to their workforce, are fair. They know their people well, understand what's important to them, when they're not performing well and when they need some space and time.

The people you lead, manage and mentor won't necessarily remember your specific achievements but they will certainly remember *how* you achieved them. That's the power of values-based leadership. It holds true whether you are a CEO or commanding a warship.

8

Culture and Communication

'Culture eats strategy for breakfast.'

Peter F. Drucker

REAR ADMIRAL LEE Goddard considers himself as much a follower as a leader. For him, leading people needs a balance of four things: leadership, management, mentoring and followership: 'I have to be a good mentor, teaching and acting by example, and I also have to be a good follower: to show how people should follow you and also how a leader should follow others. The followership is really important.' Nowhere is that concept more relevant than when it comes to a company's values and culture.

CEOs play a critical role in shaping company culture. As we've already seen, their influence can be far-reaching. The changes they make, the policies they create, and the behaviours they model all influence the way others in the organization behave and the reputation that organization has. From communicating the big-picture vision to making sure core values are embedded into day-to-day working life, CEOs need plenty of self-awareness when it comes to their impact on company culture.

But what is company culture? It can feel a bit intangible. You might know it when you see it, but be hard pressed to describe it. I like the way management guru, Roger Steare, defines it as 'the way human beings behave together – what they value and what they celebrate.'[1] Every culture is unique, but, according to John Coleman, writing in the *Harvard Business Review*,[2] it is possible to identify some common components:

Vision
A vision statement is a simple but foundational element of culture which, in turn, guides values and provides purpose. It's an essential building block.

Values
A company's values are the core of its culture. While a vision articulates a company's purpose, values offer a set of guidelines on the behaviours and mindsets needed to achieve that vision.

Practices
Values need to be enshrined in a company's practices to provide day-to-day operational principles. Walk the talk time again.

People
A coherent culture needs people who either share its core values or are willing and able to embrace those values. Get them on board or let them go.

Narrative
Being able to tell a company's unique story can really help to create and embed culture. Unearth yours and use it.

---

[1] A. Hill, 'Corporate culture: Lofty aspirations', *Financial Times*, 12 July 2012.

[2] J. Coleman, 'Six components of a great corporate culture', *Harvard Business Review*, 6 May 2013. Available from https://hbr.org/2013/05/six-components-of-culture [accessed 18 August 2020].

Place

Place – whether geography, architecture or aesthetic design – also impacts the values and behaviours of people in a workplace. Does your physical environment match your values and vision?

You may find that identifying and understanding these elements more fully in your organization might help with revitalizing or reshaping your own culture.

Values and vision: The foundations of culture

As you take leadership of the company, set the scene for the company's success in three to five years' time. Share your vision; get them on board: 'This is us in three years' time – successful, a great place to work, a good corporate citizen, an entity with a good return.'

Reverse-engineer the vision for how the company will get there. Define the values you'll embody. Defining and communicating values and vision is not a single act, a town hall meeting set piece. It's about buy-in from C-suite to shop floor. And it's about embodying them in how you behave, act and make decisions. When employees see the CEO behave in a way that demonstrates company values, it resonates and encourages them to do the same. When they see a mismatch, it tells them that their behaviour doesn't matter because the CEO is not walking the talk. Get your trusted confidants to tell you if and when you're going off-base.

Just as a team code of honour can help bind a senior management team, communicating the values that underpin company vision can help build and reinforce organizational culture across the board.

Shared company values: Some examples

- Take responsibility for your goals.

- Take collective responsibility for the outcomes achieved.

- Be loyal.

- Create a culture of respect, empathy, integrity and trust.

- Respect each other, respect the community and respect the society.

- Empathize with the demands of your team members.

- We mean what we say.

- We do the right thing.

- We trust each other and we are trusted by our stakeholders.

- Be consistent.

You'll also have a crucial role to play to make sure that organizational systems and processes are aligned in ways that reinforce the culture and values, whether that's how people are hired, how people's performance is measured and tracked or interaction with customers and suppliers.

Some people can be cynical about vision and values and culture but, in the end, they matter. If you get pushback, analyse it, take a break, disengage and come back to it. But there are good reasons to persevere. In a 2014 study,[3] Charles A. O'Reilly III and colleagues

---

[3] C. A. O'Reilly, D. F. Caldwell, J. A. Chatman and B. Doerr (2014). 'The promise and problems of organizational culture: CEO personality, culture, and firm performance'. *Group & Organization Management*, 39(6), 595–625. https://journals.sagepub.com/doi/full/10.1177/1059601114550713

at Stanford University surveyed high-tech firms in the US and Ireland. Not only did they find a link between CEO personality and culture; they also identified a link between culture and company performance. Companies with higher financial performance had cultures that emphasized adaptability and transparency, and were customer-, results- and detail-oriented. When those companies were also run by an adaptable and conscientious CEO, they were even more likely see revenue growth.

How to change your culture

You'd be a lucky CEO to walk into a company with a ready-made culture that fits perfectly with your own values and vision or that's fit for purpose for the direction in which you want to go. Just as strategy is not fixed but needs to adapt and change as internal and external circumstances dictate, so does organizational culture. It seems likely – probably sooner rather than later – that you'll want or need to effect cultural change.

In 2019, the Institute for Corporate Productivity (i4cp) surveyed more than 7,000 companies about their experiences of cultural change.[4] Two-thirds of the survey respondents said that their organizations had recently or were currently going through some form of culture change, but only 15% rated their efforts as either 'highly' or 'very highly' successful. Evidence, if any were needed, that cultural change is hard.

But you're not off the hook yet. Most (78%) survey respondents felt that any change to culture needs to be driven by the CEO, although the survey also acknowledged how crucial it can be to enlist the support of key internal influencers. Renovating an existing culture was more effective than an entire transformation. It seems that one

---

[4] i4cp, *2019 Talent predictions*. Report, 2019.

way to tackle cultural change is to figure out what's core to you, what's working and what needs to evolve and change.

Writing in the *Financial Times* in 2020,[5] the Institute's chief research officer, Kevin Martin, took a more detailed look at those successful 15% of companies. He discovered that they had undertaken a number of specific actions which not only gave them the ability to change but, like the results reported in the Stanford study, also seemed to help them achieve superior growth over the past five years, whether in revenues, customer satisfaction, market share or profitability.

Based on those actions, here are his guidelines for developing a future-ready corporate culture.

Do: Renovate, listen, explain, influence, measure

Renovation, not transformation

More than half of the organizations that were 'highly successful' in changing the culture had set out to preserve the best of the company's existing norms, values and history while also looking for new 'stretches'.

Listen to employees

Senior leaders often assume they know what the culture represents. Too often, they are wrong. Two-thirds of the successful organizations began by gathering data from the workforce and other stakeholders on how they viewed the existing culture and what they wanted the new one to be.

---

[5] K. Martin, 'How to future-proof company culture', *Financial Times*, 13 February 2020. Available from www.ft.com/content/39db7e82-3947-11ea-ac3c-f68c10993b04 [accessed 18 August 2020].

Explain what is changing and why – from the top

The CEO must articulate the company's purpose and mission, why changing the culture is vital and what it seeks to change. In 86% of the successful organizations, the chief executive met the senior leadership team first to make clear the behavioural changes that would be required.

Find the influencers and energizers, and sign them up

These people may come from across the business. More than half of the successful organizations had identified influential employees to enlist them for their perspective and as champions of cultural change. It's also important to know who your 'blockers' might be.

Plan how progress will be measured, monitored and reported

Think about pulse surveys and other feedback tools to measure progress. This important step was neglected by 90% of the organizations whose efforts to overhaul corporate culture failed.

Don't: Delegate, tolerate, underestimate

Don't delegate ownership of cultural change

The CEO must be the culture champion, using investor calls, company town hall meetings, customer meetings, visits to production facilities, media interviews and any other means at his or her disposal to discuss the importance of changing the company culture. Some organizations appoint a culture tsar or a culture committee, but what really makes the difference is the chief executive committing time and resources to take the lead.

Don't put up with leaders who resist

Their ability and willingness to embody the change is non-negotiable. It may be necessary to move naysayers and blockers out of the way.

Don't underestimate soft power

Things like culture, and leadership traits such as empathy, deep listening and vulnerability may have traditionally been seen as 'soft' but they are 'hard' in terms of business impact. Soft is the new hard.

Communication

It'll be clear by now that the CEO role demands the highest level of communication skills, both within the company and with the board, external stakeholders and the broader community. As with so much else, a CEO's communication style and ability sets the tone for communication throughout every department and every level of the company. And good communication is a constant.

George Bernard Shaw hit the nail on the head when he said: 'The biggest single problem with communication is the illusion that it has taken place.' It is important to realize that information is not communication; the ratio should be something like 80% communication to 20% information. Make no assumptions. Have clear communication channels and use them consistently. Make sure you're being heard. Just saying 'Do you agree?' is not enough; you need to solicit opinions more systematically. Just like every other aspect of the business, you need a communications *strategy*.

A communications strategy

You need a communications plan for ongoing initiatives and for specific issues, especially if they involve a change – like working towards cultural change or a new strategic plan – but you also need to get the comms right from the very start.

In the run-up to taking my first CEO role, I benefitted hugely from advice from my mentor, John Connolly, who created a first 100 days comms plan for me. He understood well how those first moments as CEO, the first things you say and do, have a major impact on setting expectations and managing relationships. There's simply not the time to get off to a bad start.

As we saw in Chapter 5, all stakeholders will attach greater meaning than usual to the words and actions of a new CEO:

- Employees will look to possible changes the CEO might make: what might it mean for me and my colleagues?
- Externally, media, analysts and investors will place greater significance on the first decision made by the CEO.
- Everyone will look for symbolic gestures and attach meaning to the CEO's values. They will compare everything the new CEO does to 'what the previous CEO would have done'. They will make judgements about what is announced as an indicator of how the CEO will perform, future company direction etc.

CEOs who manage the communication and relationships well in the first 100 days tend to have a longer honeymoon period and be given the 'benefit of the doubt' from major shareholders for longer.

CEOs that do this badly usually face pressure to demonstrate, or justify, their strategies earlier or to make significant change within the company. The case for getting the comms right is clear and unequivocal.

The communications plan needs to consider how perceptions can be moved over time and how the right positioning can move the needle. It needs to take into account how the business is currently performing; perceptions about the former CEO and his or her strategy; the external environment impacting the business; and perceptions about how the new CEO will fit in. Once those factors have been analysed, it's then possible to create a plan that looks to engage key stakeholders appropriately and in a timely way.

Stakeholder mapping

The concept of stakeholder mapping is a useful tool to identify all of your stakeholders, the interdependencies between them and priorities for communication. Because your time will be limited, this kind of mapping will help you make the right judgements about what and when to communicate to whom.

The first task is to identify all key stakeholders. For a CEO, these will include:

- the Chair and the board;
- executive team;
- other employees;
- investors;
- media and analysts;
- government and regulators;
- competitors and business associations;
- customers and suppliers.

Once your key stakeholders have been identified, you can begin to map them according to factors such as significance, influence, financial stake, emotional stake and motivations. Think about who might be your biggest supporters and who are like naysayers. You could map communication needs using a simple matrix, like this one in Figure 6, which plots levels of communication needed based on power and interest.

Once you've identified your stakeholders, and their levels of power and interest, you can create your stakeholder communications plan. This should include the details of message development and message delivery and take into account both formal and informal communication tailored to stakeholder group needs and knowledge. The aim is to anticipate and manage stakeholder perceptions, and to secure their buy-in. For example, it's important for new CEOs to meet key employees, investors and media contacts early on, as they, in turn, will communicate your key messages. Personal contact beyond this core group can then spread out based on the priorities identified in the mapping and the plan.

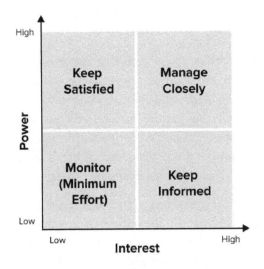

Figure 6: Stakeholder mapping matrix

Mind your investors

The appointment of a CEO is an unusual event for investors. Like other stakeholders, they'll be looking for early signs of the direction in which you'll take your organization, judging you on your successes and failures. Unlike others, they're in a position to put immediate pressure on your share price, your board and company strategy. Initial impressions investors gain will be influenced by how you're portrayed in the media, how well you're seen to make the transition, how you interact with your people and your board. Your first Annual General Meeting will be critical. Make sure your investment management and communication strategies are working as effectively as possible.

...but keep an eye on internal stakeholders too

Take steps to identify your internal stakeholders too and ensure your team members are regularly briefed on company initiatives. Within the constraints of compliance and confidentiality, be as transparent as you can. Don't have furtive meetings in conference rooms or engage in activities where the majority of people feel left out of the loop.

Adriana Giotta talks about adjusting the communication style according to the interlocutor. Some people will have more prior information than others and some will understand your messages more readily. The big picture may be obvious to you, but you have the benefit of this being your personal vision. It may not be obvious to others, and you may need to break things down into more manageable chunks that everyone can digest.

Despite your best intentions, set-piece internal communications may not be read at all; the effort of producing something, whether that's newsletters or other written material, may not be commensurate with the results you achieve. I started off writing a newsletter, but realized that about 20% of people opened it and then it was deleted within 40 seconds. Instead, I decided to make myself as approachable and transparent as I could, open to other forms – and two-way – communication as often as possible.

Aligning messages

You also need to make sure that your team is on board with agreed messages to the market and your stakeholders. Once, when I was serving on board a ship, the media were due to come on board the next day. They were being given access to any member of the ship's company. The captain briefed the entire ship's company and said: 'Please feel free to respond openly and sensibly to any questions that you may receive; remember that our mission is "to fight and win at sea".' The press representatives commented the next day that, no matter who they asked, the mission objective was exactly the same.

Table 1: A new CEO: Communication objectives, messages and perceptions: Some examples

	In advance	Day 1	Week 1	First 90 days	Year 1
Communication objectives	1. Prepare the ground 2. Manage expectations 3. Maintain good relationships while maintaining confidentiality 4. Prepare background material 5. Prepare plan	1. Smooth trouble-free announcement of appointment 2. Expectations of key stakeholders are met 3. Make enough but not big promises 4. Set the parameters against which you will be judged in the months ahead	1. Smooth trouble-free announcement of appointment 2. Start to build relationships 3. Enthusiasm for new chief	The company is on the way to a new future and we have started to deliver on stakeholder expectations	1. Confidence and positive sentiment towards the company 2. Positive comparisons with competitors

What will people want to know?	What does s/he stand for? Where does s/he want to take the company? How does s/he stack up? What constraints will there be? What will be the strategy and priorities?	Can this person deliver? 1. Background 2. Track record 3. Style/behaviour 4. Experience	What does everyone think?	Is this person on the right track? Is this person showing leadership and commanding respect? What has s/he achieved?	Is there a strong vision? Can they understand this company? Do I know where it is heading? Has s/he delivered on expectations?
Perceptions	The company has been well managed but is not performing as well as it could	The company has chosen a strong candidate who can build on strengths. S/he has: • background;	The new CEO has made a good start. S/he has: • impressed key stakeholders;	The company is in good hands and we can see progress is accelerating	This is a quality company that knows where it is going Clear understanding of direction

• track record; • style/behaviour; • experience.	• not overstated; • shown s/he has what it takes; • understood relationships.	Taking action and behaving consistently Making necessary changes Quality of leadership improving Employees engaged Culture change underway	Pride and involvement Worth investing in Want to be associated with the company

Non-verbal communication

Psychologist Albert Mehrabian's pioneering work on non-verbal communication[6] provides evidence for what we instinctively know: that our words are not the only means by which we communicate our messages. Whether or not his (in)famous 7–38–55% communication rule (that communication is 7% words, 38% tone of voice and 55% non-verbal cues – or body language) has been misquoted or misused, what's not in dispute is that your demeanour and body language matter just as much as, if not more than, what you actually say.

Navy instructors often use the phrase: 'Sirs, don't run because it frightens the troops.' And it's true that, as a leader, even the smallest non-verbal cues will be noticed, analysed and commented on. The potential for misinterpretation is high. Carry yourself in a certain way; you need to be seen as approachable, open and transparent, while keeping a fine balance between that and oversharing. Even if you are carrying the weight of the world on your shoulders, be careful not to show it.

I wish I had listened to my own advice. I've been told that I'd be a terrible poker player. My fabulous Head of Investor Relations once took me aside before a meeting and said: 'Boss, smile and nod; that is all you need to do in this analysts meeting.' I looked at her as if she had gone mad: 'What about the strategy, the numbers, the results, the vision?' I protested. 'These analysts have the power to lift or trash the share price with a single stroke of the pen,' she said. 'They will ask dumb questions, because that is what they do. I know you well enough to know that this will piss you off, and while you won't say anything, your face will give it away and we will be toast. You smile and nod; I will deal with the idiots.' She was spot on. I had to learn the hard way the importance of equanimity.

---

[6] A. Mehrabian, *Nonverbal communication*. Transaction Publishers, 1972.

Part 3

Peak #2: Running the business

9

Two Inspirational Views
of Leadership

*'Leadership is the art of accomplishing more than the science of
management says is possible.'*

Oren Harari, *The Leadership Secrets of*
Colin Powell

IT MAY SOUND tautologous to state that being a CEO is all
about being a leader. But much, of course, depends on what
we mean by leadership. What we do know these days is that it's
not just about seniority, status or hierarchy. And, as we saw in
Chapter 2, the characteristics we often associate with leaders are
no guarantee of CEO success. Perhaps that's why the shelves of
bookshops and the pages of the *Harvard Business Review* are full
of a never-ending series of viewpoints and research about what
it takes to get to the top and how to succeed when you get there.
Doubtless, we all have our personal favourites. I'd like to share
mine with you here.

Learning from a four-star general

One thing that Lee Goddard and I have in common is a set of
leadership principles we have pinned to our office walls. They
come from a business professor, Oren Harari. His subject: retired

four-star US General, Colin Powell. Harari had – by chance – found himself on a speaking platform with Powell back in 1996; he was effectively his warm-up act. Inspired by the general, he bought his autobiography, *My American Journey*. What Harari was not expecting was that the book would have what he calls 'an unexpected professional payoff'. He started to make note of the principles and words that underpinned Powell's leadership philosophy, to the extent that he was 'tempted to toss out just about every other leadership book in my library'.

Cue the article *Quotations from Chairman Powell: A Leadership Primer* and the bestselling book, *The Leadership Secrets of Colin Powell*. It's quite a story. At its core, Harari explores the foundations of Powell's leadership style, using that original framework for his leadership philosophy based on 18 quotes from Powell himself, with his own gloss on what they mean. I'm reproducing them here (in slightly edited form) in the hope that you'll find them inspirational too.

LESSON ONE

"Being responsible sometimes means pissing people off."

Good leadership involves responsibility to the welfare of the group, which means that some people will get angry at your actions and decisions. It's inevitable if you're honourable. Trying to get everyone to like you is a sign of mediocrity: You'll avoid the tough decisions, you'll avoid confronting the people who need to be confronted, and you'll avoid offering differential rewards based on differential performance because some people might get upset. Ironically, by procrastinating on the difficult choices, by trying not to get anyone mad, and by treating everyone equally "nicely" regardless of their contributions, you'll simply ensure that the only people you'll wind up angering are the most creative and productive people in the organization.

LESSON TWO

> *"The day soldiers stop bringing you their problems is the day you have stopped leading them. They have either lost confidence that you can help them or concluded that you do not care. Either case is a failure of leadership."*

If this were a litmus test, the majority of CEOs would fail. One, they build so many barriers to upward communication that the very idea of someone lower in the hierarchy looking up to the leader for help is ludicrous. Two, the corporate culture they foster often defines asking for help as weakness or failure, so people cover up their gaps, and the organization suffers accordingly. Real leaders make themselves accessible and available. They show concern for the efforts and challenges faced by underlings—even as they demand high standards. Accordingly, they are more likely to create an environment where problem analysis replaces blame.

LESSON THREE

> *"Don't be buffaloed by experts and elites. Experts often possess more data than judgment. Elites can become so inbred that they produce hemophiliacs who bleed to death as soon as they are nicked by the real world."*

Small companies and start-ups don't have the time for analytically detached experts. They don't have the money to subsidize lofty elite, either. The president answers the phone and drives the truck when necessary; everyone on the payroll visibly produces and contributes to bottom-line results or they're history. But as companies get bigger, they often forget who "brung them to the dance": things like all-hands involvement, egalitarianism, informality, market intimacy, daring, risk, speed, agility. Policies that emanate from ivory towers often have an adverse impact on the people out in the field who are fighting the wars or bringing in the revenues. Real leaders are vigilant—and combative—in the face of these trends.

LESSON FOUR

"Don't be afraid to challenge the pros, even in their own backyard."

Learn from the pros, observe them, seek them out as mentors and partners. But remember that even the pros may have levelled out in terms of their learning and skills. Sometimes even the pros can become complacent and lazy. Leadership does not emerge from blind obedience to anyone… Good leadership encourages everyone's evolution.

LESSON FIVE

"Never neglect details. When everyone's mind is dulled or distracted the leader must be doubly vigilant."

Strategy equals execution. All the great ideas and visions in the world are worthless if they can't be implemented rapidly and efficiently. Good leaders delegate and empower others liberally, but they pay attention to details, every day… Bad ones—even those who fancy themselves as progressive "visionaries"—think they're somehow "above" operational details. Paradoxically, good leaders understand something else: An obsessive routine in carrying out the details begets conformity and complacency, which in turn dulls everyone's mind. That is why even as they pay attention to details, they continually encourage people to challenge the process. They implicitly understand the sentiment that the job of a leader is not to be the chief organizer, but the chief dis-organizer.

LESSON SIX

"You don't know what you can get away with until you try."

You know the expression "it's easier to get forgiveness than permission?" Well, it's true. Good leaders don't wait for official blessing to try things out. They're prudent, not reckless. But they also realize a fact of life in most organizations: If you ask enough people for permission, you'll inevitably come up against someone who believes his job is to say "no." So the moral is, don't ask. I'm serious. In my own research with colleague Linda Mukai, we found that less effective middle managers endorsed the sentiment, "If I haven't explicitly been told 'yes,' I can't do it," whereas the good ones believed "If I haven't explicitly been told 'no,' I can." There's a world of difference between these two points of view.

LESSON SEVEN

"Keep looking below surface appearances. Don't shrink from doing so (just) because you might not like what you find."

"If it ain't broke, don't fix it" is the slogan of the complacent, the arrogant or the scared. It's an excuse for inaction, a call to non-arms. It's a mindset that assumes (or hopes) that today's realities will continue tomorrow in a tidy, linear and predictable fashion. Pure fantasy. In this sort of culture, you won't find people who proactively take steps to solve problems as they emerge. Here's a little tip: don't invest in these companies.

LESSON EIGHT

"Organization doesn't really accomplish anything. Plans don't accomplish anything, either. Theories of management don't much

matter. Endeavours succeed or fail because of the people involved.
Only by attracting the best people will you accomplish great deeds."

In a brain-based economy, your best assets are people. We've heard this expression so often that it's become trite. But how many leaders really "walk the talk" with this stuff? Too often, people are assumed to be empty chess pieces to be moved around by grand viziers, which may explain why so many top managers immerse their calendar time in deal-making, restructuring and the latest management fad. How many immerse themselves in the goal of creating an environment where the best, the brightest, the most creative are attracted, retained and—most importantly—unleashed?

LESSON NINE

"Organization charts and hence titles count for next to nothing."

Organization charts are frozen, anachronistic photos in a workplace that ought to be as dynamic as the external environment around you. If people really followed organization charts, companies would collapse. In well-run organizations, titles are also pretty meaningless. At best, they advertise some authority—an official status conferring the ability to give orders and induce obedience. But titles mean little in terms of real power, which is the capacity to influence and inspire. Have you ever noticed that people will personally commit to certain individuals who on paper (or on the org chart) possess little authority—but instead possess pizzazz, drive, expertise and genuine caring for team-mates and products? On the flip side, non-leaders in management may be formally anointed with all the perks and frills associated with high positions, but they have little influence on others, apart from their ability to extract minimal compliance to minimal standards.

LESSON TEN

> *"Never let your ego get so close to your position that when your position goes, your ego goes with it."*

Too often, change is stifled by people who cling to familiar turfs and job descriptions. One reason that even large organizations wither is that managers won't challenge old, comfortable ways of doing things. But real leaders understand that, nowadays, every one of our jobs is becoming obsolete. The proper response is to obsolete our activities before someone else does. Effective leaders create a climate where people's worth is determined by their willingness to learn new skills and grab new responsibilities, thus perpetually reinventing their jobs. The most important question in performance evaluation becomes not, "How well did you perform your job since the last time we met?" but, "How much did you change it?"

LESSON ELEVEN

> *"Fit no stereotypes. Don't chase the latest management fads. The situation dictates which approach best accomplishes the team's mission."*

Flitting from fad to fad creates team confusion, reduces the leader's credibility and drains organizational coffers. Blindly following a particular fad generates rigidity in thought and action. Sometimes speed to market is more important than total quality. Sometimes an unapologetic directive is more appropriate than participatory discussion. To quote Powell, some situations require the leader to hover closely; others require long, loose leashes. Leaders honour their core values, but they are flexible in how they execute them. They understand that management techniques are not magic mantras but simply tools to be reached for at the right times.

LESSON TWELVE

"Perpetual optimism is a force multiplier."

The ripple effect of a leader's enthusiasm and optimism is awesome. So is the impact of cynicism and pessimism. Leaders who whine and blame engender those same behaviours among their colleagues. I am not talking about stoically accepting organizational stupidity and performance incompetence with a "what, me worry?" smile. I am talking about a gung ho attitude that says "we can change things here, we can achieve awesome goals, we can be the best." Spare me the grim litany of the "realist"; give me the unrealistic aspirations of the optimist any day.

LESSON THIRTEEN

'Powell's Rules for Picking People'—Look for intelligence and judgment and, most critically, a capacity to anticipate, to see around corners. Also look for loyalty, integrity, a high energy drive, a balanced ego and the drive to get things done."

How often do our recruitment and hiring processes tap into these attributes? More often than not, we ignore them in favour of length of resume, degrees and prior titles. A string of job descriptions a recruit held yesterday seem to be more important than who one is today, what she can contribute tomorrow or how well his values mesh with those of the organization. You can train a bright, willing novice in the fundamentals of your business fairly readily, but it's a lot harder to train someone to have integrity, judgment, energy, balance and the drive to get things done. Good leaders stack the deck in their favour right in the recruitment phase.

LESSON FOURTEEN

(Borrowed by Powell from Michael Korda): "Great leaders are almost always great simplifiers, who can cut through argument, debate and doubt, to offer a solution everybody can understand."

Effective leaders understand the KISS principle, or Keep It Simple, Stupid. They articulate vivid, overarching goals and values, which they use to drive daily behaviours and choices among competing alternatives. Their visions and priorities are lean and compelling, not cluttered and buzzword-laden. Their decisions are crisp and clear, not tentative and ambiguous. They convey an unwavering firmness and consistency in their actions, aligned with the picture of the future they paint. The result? Clarity of purpose, credibility of leadership, and integrity in organization.

LESSON FIFTEEN

Part I: "Use the formula P=40 to 70, in which P stands for the probability of success and the numbers indicate the percentage of information acquired." Part II: "Once the information is in the 40 to 70 range, go with your gut."

Powell's advice is don't take action if you have only enough information to give you less than a 40 percent chance of being right, but don't wait until you have enough facts to be 100 percent sure, because by then it is almost always too late. His instinct is right: excessive delays in the name of information gathering means analysis paralysis. Procrastination in the name of reducing risk actually increases risk.

LESSON SIXTEEN

"The commander in the field is always right and the rear echelon is wrong, unless proved otherwise."

Too often, the reverse defines corporate culture. This is one of the main reasons why leaders like Ken Iverson of Nucor Steel, Percy Barnevik of Asea Brown Boveri, and Richard Branson of Virgin have kept their corporate staffs to a bare-bones minimum... Shift the power and the financial accountability to the folks who are bringing in the beans, not the ones who are counting or analyzing them.

LESSON SEVENTEEN

"Have fun in your command. Don't always run at a breakneck pace. Take leave when you've earned it. Spend time with your families."

Corollary: "Surround yourself with people who take their work seriously, but not themselves, those who work hard and play hard."... Seek people who have some balance in their lives, who are fun to hang out with, who like to laugh (at themselves, too) and who have some non-job priorities which they approach with the same passion that they do their work. Spare me the grim workaholic or the pompous pretentious "professional;" I'll help them find jobs with my competitor.

LESSON EIGHTEEN

"Command is lonely."

Harry Truman was right. Whether you're a CEO or the temporary head of a project team, the buck stops here. You can encourage participative management and bottom-up employee involvement, but ultimately, the essence of leadership is the willingness to make the tough, unambiguous choices that will have an impact on the fate of the organization. I've seen too many non-leaders flinch from this responsibility. Even as you create an informal, open, collaborative corporate culture, prepare to be lonely.

Justin Menkes' executive intelligence

It's interesting that Colin Powell's thirteenth lesson talks about 'intelligence and judgment, and, most critically, a capacity to anticipate, to see around corners'. Brainpower is very much to the fore for Justin Menkes, whose work on executive intelligence looks beyond the traditional cognitive measure – IQ – to identify the applied business intelligence needed to excel as a CEO.

I'm drawn to Menkes' ideas because I've never been one to assume that leaders are born, not made, nor that personality and style can give a true indication of leadership success. Menkes is firmly in the camp that believes that too much emphasis has been given to personality and style and too little to types of intelligence that enhance leadership performance: 'Personality is not a differentiator of star talent. It is an individual's facility for clear thinking or intelligence that largely determines their leadership success.'[1] This executive intelligence is the ability to digest, often with the help of others, large amounts of information in order to form important decisions that produce useful action with the right amount of deliberation.

Executive intelligence is related to, but not the same as, academic intelligence. For Menkes, academic aptitude in things measured by IQ tests – such as language, maths and spatial reasoning – have little relevance to many of the day-to-day demands of business. IQ tests only measure a fraction of a person's cognitive abilities. Business is not just about generating ideas, but translating those ideas into results. It's often about practical, on-your-feet thinking skills. Specifically, business leaders must excel in three areas:

1. Accomplishing the tasks of leadership
2. Working with and through people
3. Evaluating their own attitudes and behaviours, and making adjustments when necessary

---

[1] J. Menkes, *Executive intelligence: What all great leaders have.* Collins, 2006.

Note that, once again, high-end interpersonal skills and self-management and awareness are to the fore – this time alongside problem solving and critical thinking skills.

In an article in *Harvard Business Review* in 2005,[2] Menkes identifies the skills that make up executive intelligence in these areas:

Regarding tasks, intelligent leaders:

- appropriately define a problem and differentiate essential objectives from less relevant concerns;
- anticipate obstacles to achieving their objectives and identify sensible means to circumvent them;
- critically examine the accuracy of underlying assumptions;
- articulate the strengths and weaknesses of the suggestions or arguments posed;
- recognize what is known about an issue, what more needs to be known, and how best to obtain the relevant and accurate information needed;
- use multiple perspectives to identify probable unintended consequences of various action plans.

Regarding people, intelligent leaders:

- recognize the conclusions that can be drawn from a particular exchange;
- recognize the underlying agendas and motivations of individuals and groups involved in a situation;
- anticipate the probable reactions of individuals to actions or communications;
- accurately identify the core issues and perspectives that are central to a conflict;

---

[2] J. Menkes, 'Hiring for smarts', *Harvard Business Review*, November 2005. Available from https://hbr.org/2005/11/hiring-for-smarts [accessed 18 August 2020].

- appropriately consider the probable effects and possible unintended consequences that may result from taking a particular course of action;
- acknowledge and balance the different needs of all relevant stakeholders.

Regarding themselves, intelligent leaders:

- pursue feedback that may reveal errors in their judgements and make appropriate adjustments;
- recognize their personal biases or limitations in perspective and use this understanding to improve their thinking and their action plans;
- recognize when serious flaws in their ideas or actions require swift public acknowledgement of mistakes and a dramatic change in direction;
- appropriately articulate the essential flaws in others' arguments and reiterate the strengths in their own positions;
- recognize when it is appropriate to resist others' objections and remain committed to a sound course of action.

In practice then, great leaders not only conceptualize and formulate strategy, but also see initiatives through to completion. This requires them to make adjustments based on new information or early results, understand challenges and potential consequences, ask thoughtful questions and probe the assumptions of others. These are the clear thinkers who surround themselves with like-minded people, can get rapidly to the heart of the matter and have the confidence and self-awareness to change tack if needs be.

10

Strategy

'The value of a strategy is inversely related to the number of pages required to express it.'

Donald Sull,
MIT Sloan School of Management

THE SECOND PEAK a CEO must scale often receives less attention than the two peaks on either side. As we've seen, stakeholders often get caught up in the anticipation and reality of the first 100 days. And, as we'll see, at the other end, an outgoing CEO's record and legacy will also be subject to major scrutiny. In the middle, CEOs will be getting on with the central years of their tenure – the time for building on early success and impact, shifting priorities, evolving new ways of working. Early work on vision and values will transform into full-blown strategic plans that will need to be properly implemented when the CEO truly takes responsibility for the direction of the company. And it's a time for running the business.

Research by consultants from Korn Ferry and McKinsey[1] looked specifically at this crucial second peak by identifying and

---

[1] R. Zemmel, M. Cuddihy and D. Carey, 'How successful CEOs manage their middle act', *Harvard Business Review*, May–June 2018. Available from https://hbr.org/2018/05/how-successful-ceos-manage-their-middle-act [accessed 18 August 2020].

interviewing almost 150 top CEOs about how their priorities, mindsets and approaches to leadership had evolved mid-tenure, what they had focused on and what they wish they had done differently. Interestingly for our three-peak approach, many of the CEOs interviewed hadn't consciously thought about their tenure in terms of phases, but after reflecting on their approaches recognized that it did have distinct acts, with 'significant differences between the early phases of the CEO run, the middle term, and the latter stages'.

It was in this middle term that the highest-performing CEOs made a conscious decision to re-examine the company's context, reassess their agenda and continue to actively shape the organization and strategy. Five themes emerged as essential to success in leaders' middle years:

- The importance of resetting ambitions to avoid losing momentum
- The need to attack silos and fix broken processes
- The imperative of rejuvenating leadership talent
- The value of building internal and external mechanisms for dissent and disruptive ideas
- The need to double-down on bold moves that could help the company succeed over a long horizon

In short, these were not leaders that were standing still, enjoying the view from the top of their first peak. They were facing up to the challenges of peak #2, constantly reviewing themselves, their organizations and what they needed to do. Precisely how they spent their time changed too. Figure 7 is an interesting summary of how their priorities had shifted and changed.

	LESS TIME THAN PREVIOUSLY	SAME	MORE
Strategy/Strategic moves	6%	31%	63%
R&D/Long-term investments	31		69
Organizational change	33	33	33
M&A/Transactions	19	63	19
Business performance reviews	25	69	6
External stakeholder interactions	44		56
Board interactions	33	33	33
Succession planning	12		88
Broader talent planning	23		77

NOTE BECAUSE OF ROUNDING, SOME CATEGORIES DO NOT ADD UP TO 100%.
FROM "HOW SUCCESSFUL CEOS MANAGE THEIR MIDDLE ACT," BY RODNEY ZEMMEL ET AL., MAY–JUNE 2018 © HBR.ORG

Figure 7: How CEOs spend their time during Peak #2[2]

Getting strategy right

Crucially, mid-term CEOs were spending 63% more time than previously on strategy and strategic moves. That's what the rest of this chapter is going to focus on: what strategy is and how it's formulated, communicated, implemented and monitored. Essentially, a CEO plans for growth, survival or exit, and most probably all of the above at some stage. Getting strategy right is a fundamental and essential task for CEOs and the organizations they run. From the moment you start in your role (or even before that) you need to give some thought to the company's future direction, recognizing that this will change as you learn more and find yourself affected by the vagaries of the business environment. You need a strategic plan.

---

[2] R. Zemmel, M. Cuddihy and D. Carey, 'How successful CEOs manage their middle act', *Harvard Business Review*, May–June 2018. Available from https://hbr.org/2018/05/how-successful-ceos-manage-their-middle-act [accessed 18 August 2020].

At its simplest, a strategic plan is a roadmap, designed to show how the company can get from A (meaning where we are right now) to B (where we want to be). A strategy is defined by periods of time and is particularly critical as a CEO moves from the fact-finding and analysis of the first 100 days to the beginning of peak #2.

I like management guru Henry Mintzberg's definition of strategy as 'A pattern in a series of decisions'[3] because it shows that strategy is not a fixed result, but dynamic, evolutionary and emergent. Strategy is not one decision; it must be viewed in the context of a number of decisions and the interrelationships between them.

According to professor of strategy, Freek Vermeulen,[4] what we often consider to be strategies are really just goals, such as: 'We want to be market-leaders in this sector.' A real strategy involves a clear set of *choices* that define what you're going to do and what you're not going to do, make sense in terms of strategic direction and can be communicated to, and understood by, both internal and external stakeholders. According to Vermeulen, many strategies fail because these choices aren't clear and are based on a top-down approach that allows little room for autonomy experimentation along the way: 'Execution involves change. Embrace it.'

Deliberate versus emergent strategy

Mintzberg is also responsible for identifying the idea of deliberate versus emergent strategy. When a *deliberate strategy* is realized, the results match the intended course of action. *Emergent strategy*

---

[3] H. Mintzberg (1987). 'The strategy concept 1: Five P's for strategy'. *California Management Review*, 30(1), 11–24.

[4] F. Vermeulen, 'Many strategies fail because they're not actually strategies', *Harvard Business Review*, 8 November 2017. Available from https://hbr.org/2017/11/many-strategies-fail-because-theyre-not-actually-strategies [accessed 18 August 2020].

emerges over time as intentions collide with and accommodate a changing reality.

For Mintzberg, deliberate strategy is important for measuring progress and benchmarks, but it's one side of the coin, the planning side. It provides the organization with a sense of purposeful direction. Emergent strategy deals with the other side of the coin, the action side, the adaptability side, the side that gets to grips with unintended consequences and emergencies. It's based on the idea that, to paraphrase Prussian Chief of Staff, Helmuth von Moltke, 'no battle plan ever survives contact with the enemy.' Mintzberg and colleagues describe the need for emergent strategy like this: 'Setting out on a predetermined course in unknown waters is the perfect way to sail straight into an iceberg.'[5]

Few, if any, business strategies are purely deliberate, just as few are purely emergent. Mixing the deliberate and the emergent strategies helps an organization to plot and control its course while also allowing for adjustments along the way. Mintzberg and colleagues again: 'All real-world strategies need to mix these in some way: to exercise control while fostering learning. Strategies, in other words, have to form as well as be formulated.'[6]

An analogy for the relationship between deliberate versus emergent strategy is found in a 2018 study by the Boston Consulting Group (BCG).[7] In a survey of 2,500 global public companies, BCG found that only 2% consistently outperformed on both growth and profitability during good and bad times. The foundation of these companies' success was their ability to renew themselves by

---

[5] H. Mintzberg, B. Ahlstrand and J. B. Lampel, *Strategy safari: The complete guide through the wilds of strategic management* (2nd ed.). Pearson Education Limited, 2009, p. 15.

[6] Mintzberg, Ahlstrand and Lampel, *Strategy safari*, p. 11.

[7] K. Haanæs, M. Reeves and J. Wurlod, 'The 2% company', BCG Henderson Institute. Available from www.bcg.com/en-gb/publications/2018/2-percent-company [accessed 18 August 2020].

driving innovation and efficiency *simultaneously*. Like deliberate and emergent strategy, these activities might be seen as contradictory, but achieving in both exploration (new ideas and innovation) and exploitation (operational proficiency and efficiency) was a precursor to balancing growth and profitability. As with emergent strategy, these 2% of companies were able to embrace disruption and renew for the future, while also maintaining their existing core operations.

The key components of a strategy

Determine the goal

Priorities and aims; why are you here; what have you been doing well and badly; what lessons have you learnt; what do you need to do to survive and thrive; where and who do you want to be?

Set a timeline. It needs to be flexible and dynamic, but with key decision (go/no-go) dates and rigid accountabilities. Otherwise, it will drift.

List the 'knowns'

Conduct:

- an appraisal of the capabilities of your people (this includes who to trust and who not to); the experiential and developmental assistance they need and by when to meet the rigours of their new or expanded roles;
- an appraisal of the capability of your company;
- an appraisal of the environment in which your company is operating;
- an honest 'gap analysis' using internal as well as trusted external sources.

Set strategic choices

To make effective strategic choices, organizations need to consider clear and easily communicated answers to the following questions:

Strategic intent: the five key choices:

1. Aspirations and goals
2. Where to play
3. How to win
4. Capabilities to build
5. Management systems to facilitate operations

Organization identity

- Purpose (Why are we here?)
- Vision (What do we want to be?)
- Mission (What is our present state and how do we get where we need to be?)
- Values (What face do we present to our stakeholders and the broader community?)

Identify critical success factors

The key performance indicators (KPIs) for achieving your strategic plan will need to encompass important targets such as:

- financial metrics, such as profit and loss, sales by region, return on investment, days' sales outstanding;
- customer metrics, such as cost of acquisition, lifetime value, retention and satisfaction rates;
- employee metrics, such as turnover, rate of response to situations vacant advertising, satisfaction.

Success is about perception and reputation too

Be regarded as a preferred employer

Being placed on the list of favourable places to work gives you a distinct advantage. The market will recognize that you are looking after your team, and the likelihood that the best-qualified employees will be attracted to your organization will increase. Incorporate ways to attract and retain motivated, engaged staff into your strategy, because the competitiveness of your company will be determined by the creativity, teamwork and motivation of your employees working together towards a common goal.

Become recognized as a good corporate citizen

When you are a leading proponent of environmental, social and governance (ESG) criteria you will become recognized as a good corporate citizen. This is not just a good thing in its own right; it will also potentially attract more investors or employees who are motivated by a wider range of criteria.

In short, and in the words of Vermeulen, strategy is 'a set of choices, that in combination lead to a coherent pattern in an organization's actions causing the creation and exploitation of competitive advantage.'[8]

Remember that a successful strategy can only be enacted on a solid base. If you are focused on what the company could and should be doing and ignore what's happening today, you might not have a future. Take time to establish a solid platform. Then you can go deeper into the critical aspects of the strategic plan. Thinking about strategy in phases – just like your CEO tenure – can help.

The Three Peaks Strategy Model

We've identified that a strategy is a road map, that it needs to blend the more deliberate with the emergent, and that it's about choices. How, then, might you as CEO approach the crucial task of setting

---

[8] F. Vermeulen, 'Many strategies fail because they're not actually strategies', *Harvard Business Review*, 8 November 2017. Available from https://hbr.org/2017/11/many-strategies-fail-because-theyre-not-actually-strategies [accessed 18 August 2020].

the direction for your own company? Just as our Three Peaks model breaks down a CEO tenure into three distinct phases, so too can your approach to strategy mirror the phases of your time as CEO using the Three Peaks Strategy Model.

Figure 8: The Three Peaks Strategy Model

Near-term strategy

Deal with the issues that can't wait

The first peak reflects the near term, lasting from your first 100 days into your first term in role. At this stage, you'll need to deal with the critical issues that can't wait: poor staff morale; changes in environmental legislation with which you need to comply; a lack of a safety culture; declining revenues or rising costs; investor dissatisfaction. If you don't deal with these immediately, there may not be any mid to long term to worry about.

I had a particularly vexatious shareholder who had inveigled his way into the organization and was giving unsolicited advice to my team. I warned him off, and within a week of my appointment he was threatening to sue the company and me personally. Perfect! That gave me the opportunity I needed to ban him from the premises in order to protect us from the potential suit and instruct the staff not to have any interaction with him. It was the perfect opportunity to rid ourselves from an annoying, dangerous distraction and, in the process, show leadership.

Identify where your company is today

Based on extensive discussion with all stakeholders, the board, investors and senior management, identify where the company is today:

- What is the competitive set?
- What do your investors and clients/customers need from you?
- Where in the economic cycle are you?

Conduct a gap analysis

Conduct a gap analysis to identify what capacities you're lacking; from where your specific issues are emanating; and where the organization is deficient. Gaps could be as simple as not having a personal development plan for each employee to not spending enough on capital expenditure. Think what you'll need to do to close the gap. Be brutal with yourself; if you aren't, the market will be. Identify where you are deficient: what do you need to do to rectify the situation and which capabilities and tools do you already have, or will need to develop, to do so.

The one to three-year strategy

The next strategy to be devised, symbolically called the second peak, is the one to three-year plan. At the outset, that's a mountain you know is there, but can't see. This is where your strategy will need to be dynamic to meet the ever-changing needs of your market.

Your internal assessment of your company, its capabilities and potential will need to be benchmarked against the external business environment in which you operate, and how issues currently facing your industry might impact or potentially impact your business. Be aware of the economic environment and assess where you are in the business cycle. Think about what steps you can take to benefit from it or protect yourself against it.

The military analogy of indicators and warnings is useful here. In military terms, an indicator is a movement of troops and materiel; a warning is strident rhetoric from the other side. If one is joined with the other, there's a clear indication that something could be about to happen; you need to take steps to prepare for it. In the commercial world, develop an awareness of what your own specific indicators and warnings might be so that, when the lights start to flash red, you are ready.

In short, the plan needs to be holistic, dealing with what you know and what you think you know, as well as encompassing your aspirations for the company.

The future

The third peak is a strategy for the future, which incorporates global, macro and microeconomic trends. Your strategy needs to look for these trends and assess their impact on your business or the business of your clients. You need to develop a plan for mitigating any negative impact and benefitting from positive changes. In order to ensure your company does not become obsolete, you need to take steps to future-proof it. This involves anticipating what is likely to happen in the future and taking action to minimize any negative impact on, or to enhance any positive opportunities for, the business. It also means recognizing broader trends, both in your industry and around it. It may mean being prepared to be geographically or sectorally diverse. And it means keeping on top of the increasingly rapid changes in technology.

Assess what trends are influencing your industry

Assess trends to identify if the main issues are things that you can safely ignore or whether you need to take them into consideration, based on where the company will be in three to five years. Incorporate important trends into your strategy.

Recognize their potential impact

The question you need to ask yourself is: 'Is this business model sustainable, on all fronts?' If not, the strategy you create needs to encompass industry trends.

For example, in the real estate sector, the co-working model (which calls for buildings to be leased on a daily or weekly basis, as people's needs fluctuate) has been in the ascendancy. Five years ago, co-working as we now know it didn't really exist; now it's a critical part of the real estate environment. As a business leader, you've got to keep an eye on the newest things and try to work out how they will affect your industry and your company. Use your experience and ability to work out whether they are a short-term 'fad' or an industry-changing trend.

Sail your own boat

You need to be aware of what other companies are doing when developing strategy for success, but you need to trust yourself too. You might all be on the same journey, but you aren't all on the same path.

Think of a yacht race. Some yachts are faster, lighter and nimbler; others have better, more talented crews. They all have the same objective: to get from the starting point to the finishing line first. As they race, progress is dependent on a number of things: how well prepared the yacht and crew are, what obstacles or advantages each one encounters. Some might change direction as they tack around an obstacle. Others might not face that obstacle so can keep on their intended course. Some might deviate from their course to catch a favourable wind shift or current; others might not sense that wind or elect to maintain their own heading.

Now translate that to the world of business. Think of each company as a yacht crewed by a team of people with varying abilities. All of the yachts have the same objective: to survive whatever is thrown at them and to get across the finish in synch with their strategic plan.

As you are sailing, negotiating the various obstacles you face and trying to be a winner in the race of competing with other companies (or at the very least, not a loser), be confident in your own abilities and those of your team. You will likely see companies changing direction, tacking because they need to avoid an issue, and you may happen to be in a better market position by luck or coincidence. There'll still be obstacles around your boat – just not the same ones.

Be aware of what other people are doing, but also realize that you don't have to slavishly follow the crowd. Use your knowledge, skill and ability to assess whether copying a competitor would benefit you. If it would, go ahead. If it wouldn't, or if you sense an advantage by taking a different route, do that instead.

Securing stakeholder approval

Once you and your team have completed your research and devised a draft strategy, you can go to your board and other stakeholders and seek to gain their approval and buy-in. Make sure you stress that your strategy will be ever-evolving, and that you'll be able to demonstrate, over time, that you will take any concerns they raise into consideration and have processes in place to mitigate and manage them.

Stakeholder approval for strategy is not a given. You have to demonstrate that it is based on sound evidence, not hopes and wishes. You may need to take on any concerns and issues they may have. Above all, you need to take them with you, especially if what you're proposing represents a significant change.

One example of this was the time I came to the conclusion that we needed to take our company offshore, due to the competitive nature of our small, tightly held market. If we didn't grow organically, we were going to be the raw end of someone else's industry consolidation plan. The majority of our competitors weren't set up to do this or had failed miserably in previous attempts; the industry didn't like the idea and, unsurprisingly, neither did my board. However, my research into the market, where we were in the economic cycle and limited opportunities for domestic growth convinced me that we needed to be in the vanguard, to become a market leader or risk getting lost in the pack.

As a senior management team, we spent a lot of time demonstrating the benefits of our plan, including the advantages and problems associated with having overseas-based assets, calculating detailed cost benefit analyses and presenting them to the board. We dealt with currency issues, timing issues and market perception issues. By laying the groundwork and doing our homework, we ultimately got the board to approve the strategy.

But that was just the start. We also had to convince a sceptical market that we were prepared and equipped to enact the strategy. By recognizing that stakeholder approval is a critical part of the strategy, we were prepared to deal with stakeholders taking sides. For example, some of the investors didn't want us to take the company offshore, and sold their shares. Others agreed with the strategy and were supportive. Still more adopted a wait-and-see approach, giving us the ability to prove our competency and win their trust. [As a side note, most of our competitors at the time have either been merged or now have an offshore strategy. Indeed, it is now part of the industry's expectations that part of the portfolio is international, reinforcing the notion that if you are right at the wrong time, you may still be wrong.]

Delivering the right messages to the market, at the right time, is also crucial. As we saw in Chapter 8, the market will be waiting for the new CEO to come up with the revised strategy. Don't disappoint; you need to inform the market what you are going to do and when. But, even more importantly, don't go to the market unprepared. The last thing you want is to have to conduct and communicate frequent strategic reviews as you adjust your flawed strategy when more relevant information comes to light. Nothing is more guaranteed to negatively impact the perception of the capabilities of senior management.

We'll look in more detail at the importance of communicating strategy below but, for now, remember that your staff are also key stakeholders and will be crucial to how strategic plans are executed. Always involve staff as much as possible in the company's strategic direction and plan, and update them regularly on progress. Seek to assuage concerns by actively engaging and communicating the plan to ensure alignment. Don't impose the strategy but rather make sure that all members of the team have had the opportunity to have a say and that their thoughts have been taken into consideration, even if the outcome is not as they had hoped.

Executing strategy

We've established that a strategy is a framework that guides the creation of a set of choices. The thinking and data analysis that underpins those choices is crucial, but for that strategy to be effectively executed, it needs to be easily communicated, remembered and acted upon by everyone in the organization.

Writing in the *MIT Sloan Management Review* in 2017, strategy expert Donald Sull and colleagues agree that strategy is about choice: 'Most winning strategies are based on a bundle of choices about, among other things, the customers to serve, the scope of the business, product offerings, and capabilities that interact with one another to help a company make money.'[9] This article also reports on his research into why so many companies find it hard to execute the strategic choices that they make.

The problem for Sull and colleagues is that, while strategy is inherently complex, executing it requires simplicity: strategies need to be simple enough for leaders at every level of the organization to understand, communicate and remember them. They need to provide concrete guidance while – as we've seen – leaving managers enough flexibility to take advantage of new opportunities, mitigate unexpected risks and adapt to changing conditions.

Identifying and communicating simple strategic choices, however, is easier said than done, especially for organizations that do not focus on a single business, have multiple types of customers or operate in less stable markets. The answer, for Sull and colleagues, is to develop a small set of strategic priorities that everyone can get behind to produce results. The priorities should be 'forward-looking and action-oriented and should focus attention on the handful of choices that matter most to the organization's success over the next few years'.

His checklist of the seven characteristics of effective strategic priorities will help you craft strategic priorities that will set a shared strategic agenda for your organization.

---

[9] D. Sull, S. Turconi, C. Sull and J. Yoder, 'Turning strategy into results', *MIT Sloan Management Review*, 28 September 2017. Available from https://sloanreview.mit.edu/article/turning-strategy-into-results/ [accessed 18 August 2020].

Limit objectives to a handful

Limiting strategic priorities focuses on what matters most and can serve as a forcing mechanism to drive difficult trade-offs among conflicting objectives.

Focus on the mid-term

Strategic priorities typically require three to five years to accomplish. Annual goals are too tactical, and longer-term goals too abstract to provide concrete guidance.

Pull towards the future

Strategic priorities should focus on initiatives that position the company to succeed in the future, not reinforce business models or strategies that worked in the past.

Make the hard calls

Strategy is about choice, and strategic priorities should tackle head-on the most consequential and difficult trade-offs facing the company.

Address critical vulnerabilities

Strategic priorities should address the elements of the strategy that are most important for success and most likely to fail in execution.

Provide concrete guidance

This should be concrete enough that leaders throughout the organization could use the strategic priorities to decide what to focus on, what not to do, and what to stop doing.

Align the top team

Strategic priorities should provide a framework for how the company as a whole will succeed. To do so, they must be agreed upon by all members of the top leadership team.

Communicating strategy

There is no point in having even the best strategic plan in the world if it's not properly communicated. It may sound obvious, but there's often a surprising mismatch between a CEO's assumptions about how well a strategy has been communicated and the reality on the ground. More research from Donald Sull and his colleagues at the MIT Strategic Agility Project throws light on this issue.[10]

Four critical strategy communication challenges

1. Senior leaders don't know that a communication problem exists

Most top managers think that the communication of strategy is fine, but less than one-third actually understand it themselves. While 97% of key managers said they were clear about strategy, only a fraction of them could actually list three of their organization's top five strategic objectives.

2. The top team disagrees on what the key priorities are

For the typical organization studied, only just over half of senior executives converged on the same list of strategic objectives.

3. The top team does not explain priorities to direct reports

It is no surprise that understanding strategy decays as it cascades down throughout an organization, but the research in the article by Sull and colleagues showed that – surprisingly – the strongest difference is from top team members to their direct reports.

---

[10] D. Sull, C. Sull and J. Yoder, 'No one knows your strategy — not even your top leaders', *MIT Sloan Management Review*, 12 February 2018. Available from https://sloanreview.mit.edu/article/no-one-knows-your-strategy-not-even-your-top-leaders/ [accessed 18 August 2020].

Table 2: Respondents by level able to identify at least three of their company's top five strategic objectives

Top team member	51%
Senior executives	22%
Middle managers	18%
Frontline supervisor	13%

4. Leaders throughout the organization do not explain why strategic objectives matter

More than half of survey respondents believed that goals had been badly or insufficiently communicated, whether in relation to their team or the company as a whole.

Table 3: How respondents' bosses explain why their goals matter

Why they matter for company and our team	46%
Why they matter for our team only	39%
Rarely explains why our goals matter	9%
Struggles to explain why our goals matter	7%

How to communicate strategy effectively

To counter these problems, Sull and his colleagues identified six steps for effectively communicating strategy throughout an organization – and, crucially, to their external stakeholders:[11]

---

[11] D. Sull, S. Turconi and C. Sull, 'Six steps to communicating strategic priorities effectively', *MIT Sloan Management Review*, 19 January 2018. Available from https://sloanreview.mit.edu/article/six-steps-to-communicating-strategic-priorities-effectively/ [accessed 18 August 2020].

1. *Limit strategic priorities to a handful*

A narrow set of clear objectives shows that the top leaders have done the hard work of making trade-offs among competing objectives, signalling a joint commitment to those objectives. Less is more here: a handful of strategic priorities makes it easier for both internal and external stakeholders to assess what matters most to the company.

2. *Provide a concise explanation of what a priority means*

There's no need to overdo things, but you do need to provide concise descriptions of what you mean by your objectives. The words 'international expansion' won't, on their own, mean very much.

3. *Clarify how a priority will be accomplished*

Giving concrete examples of how strategic priorities will be achieved is another way of establishing their credibility.

4. *Explain why a priority matters*

Clarifying the 'why' behind the 'what' will help to communicate why strategic priorities matter.

5. *Measure progress towards achieving the priority*

Clear metrics, like cost reductions, new product launches or market share, also improve credibility.

6. *Set specific targets for the future*

Setting concrete targets make the priorities real.

Managing potential loss, not change

People often resist strategic change not because of the changes *per se*, but because they fear potential loss. This might manifest itself as loss of identity, competence, comfort, reputation, time, status, security, power, independence or resources.

The successful management and communication of strategic change means managing those fears, giving enough context to make the change seem necessary and worthwhile. You will need to help people move through their perceptions of potential loss to a new productive place. The goal is to identify individuals and teams that may be especially discomforted by a new challenge and help them to tolerate that discomfort.

Communicating change

Change management specialists Prosci have identified five key tools to support the effective communication of strategic change:[12]

1. *Communication plan*

Aims to develop a general awareness of the strategic change throughout the organization, including why change is necessary and what it will look like.

2. *Sponsorship roadmap*

Identifies key sponsors (senior leaders) to support the strategy, and outlines what actions are needed from them.

3. *Coaching plan*

The link between supervisors and frontline employees – ensures that strategic objectives can be transferred and understood throughout the whole organization.

4. *Training plan*

Training is an intervention to build skills and capabilities.

---

[12] Prosci, 'Five levers of change management'. Available from www.prosci.com/resources/articles/five-levers-of-organizational-change-management [accessed 18 August 2020].

5. *Resistance management plan*

Identifies individuals/teams/groups who might resist change, and considers strategies to overcome resistance in advance.

Communication plan

Employees are often not opposed to new strategies. However, they might resist change because no one has made a clear and compelling case for why the change is needed. Achieving buy-in and acceptance from employees is the first step towards the successful adoption of strategic priorities.

Successful communication presents the right messages at the right time, in the right channel format, from the right sender. The goal is for *all* employees to understand the nature of the strategy and why it is necessary.

The following checklist outlines the essential components of a communication plan:

✓ What are the key messages?

Employees need to understand both the 'what?' and the 'why?' of strategic change, for example:

- 'Why is the change happening?'
- 'What is the risk of not changing?'
- 'What does the new strategy look like?'

✓ Who are the key audiences?

Who needs to receive the information?

✓ What do they need to know?'

Consider questions like: 'What do they currently care about?' and 'How will the strategy affect them?'

Most importantly, it needs to answer 'What's in it for me?' That's what will create the desire for change in advance.

✓ What communication channels should we use?

Successful communication needs multiple, effective ways to reach the audience. Leaders should consider a full range, including: town hall meetings; one-on-ones; newsletters; company-wide presentations; brainstorming workshops; and online forums.

✓ How will the key message be delivered?

Key messages need to be repeated five to seven times for them to stick. The delivery structure should consider face-to-face communication wherever possible, and use 'preferred senders' (see below) to deliver the message throughout the organization.

✓ How will we provide opportunities for exchange?

Create opportunities for two-way communication. Having the opportunity to share concerns, give feedback and ask questions increases the likelihood of acceptance and provides an opportunity to get ahead of any resistance before it becomes a problem.

✓ How will we prepare our 'preferred senders'?

Anyone communicating strategic change must be able to deliver effective communication and have the necessary conversations. Complete alignment is crucial.

✓ How will you measure if the communication has been effective?

Use assessment tools to evaluate how effectively messages have been communicated. Identify when communication has been ineffective, when messages are misinterpreted, or when individuals have been left behind.

Sponsorship roadmap

Prosci's research has identified that effective sponsorship is the number one contributor to successful strategic change. Change needs champions, the sponsors who will build the desire of every employee to participate and support the strategic change. Sponsors play three crucial roles:

1. Being seen to be actively and visibly participating in the change
2. Building the coalition of support with other senior leaders and managers
3. Communicating directly with employees about the business reasons and nature of the change

And, for Prosci, there are two crucial types of sponsors that employees want to hear from:

*   the CEO, to communicate the overall vision;
*   their line managers, who can follow up with more details about how the change might impact them personally.

Coaching plan

Successful change relies on the relationship between employees and their managers. These managers have a crucial role to play in communicating strategic change to their teams. They have the ability to control and filter messaging, especially about how change will impact employees. Their attitudes immediately affect how employees will react to change. Managers also play a crucial role in identifying and managing sources of resistance. They can also make or break implementation by providing positive recognition and reinforcement.

It's important, therefore, to invest the time, resources and energy into engaging and empowering managers to be good coaches and to build their own personal competency to lead change. A coaching plan should:

*   identify the network of coaches (managers) throughout the organization;
*   train and prepare them to understand and commit to understanding the reasons for change, as well as their role;

- structure both group and individual coaching sessions to engage their teams.

Training plan

In the absence of a holistic approach to change management, training is sometimes used without other critical activities like sponsorship and coaching. One of the biggest errors a team can make when introducing a change is to simply send employees to training. This is poor change management.

You need to identify the skills and capabilities that employees require and to recognize any gaps in training – and don't forget to include training for the sponsors and coaches. Training is focused on building knowledge. But, on its own, it's not enough. Training is an important part of creating successful change, but it must come after sufficient awareness and desire.

Resistance management plan

Resistance to any change is a natural reaction, but there are steps that organizations can take to prevent and mitigate its impact. Leaders should identify what resistance might look like and where it is likely to come from based on past experience and the nature of the change. They should also anticipate likely objections in advance, and create a resistance plan to counter them. Above all, it is important to identify the root cause of resistance when it does emerge during a change, whether it's an individual, team, department or specific incident.

11

Managing Yourself and Your Time

'The key is in not spending time, but in investing it.'

Stephen R. Covey

NOW THAT YOU'RE facing your second leadership peak, the honeymoon period of your first 100 days may seem way behind you. While you can look back with satisfaction at the peak you've left behind, the complexities of the job – and the resilience you'll need to face them longer term – now loom larger than ever. This is a marathon, not a sprint. As we saw in Chapter 1, carving out time to balance all of the elements of a CEO job is one of the biggest challenges you'll face. And you'll need to do this while also making sure you continue to look after yourself. From the moment you take over, the focus is on you as the CEO. You need to work out how to protect yourself in a complex and unyielding environment.

Adriana Giotta is also clear about another aspect of the role: that leadership is not a popularity contest. With so many stakeholder interests to manage and juggle, CEOs will inevitably face resentment, distrust and even hatred as part of the job. That may sound harsh, but as your thinking will generally be ahead of others, based on information they won't have or have had time to digest, people can't yet see what you can see – and that often leads to either defensiveness or attack. Being under this level of scrutiny and pressure takes some getting used to. It also means that, more than ever, you need to look after yourself and manage your time to give yourself the space just to let it all go.

Letting it go: Self-care is crucial

The techniques we discussed in Chapter 3 for self-care and resilience building will be more important than ever. I discovered that I had to make the time and space to let go, to switch off and recharge. My happy places – whether cooking, paddling or flying helicopters – became even more important to me. When I step out to pre-flight a helicopter, I don't think about work. I'm focused on checking the chopper's mechanics; I check the weather forecast and I plan what I am going to do if I hit bad weather or any other issue crops up. I immerse myself in something beyond the day job. Just as a helicopter has limited fuel, so do you. Calculate the fuel flow and plan accordingly.

Confidants, mentors and peers will also play a central role. The press, your co-workers or your own self-doubt can bring you down and it's important to have access to people with solutions to help you get back up, or who can at least provide a sounding board for your ideas. My Board of Lev became invaluable during this period of my CEO tenures. They provided a non-judgemental forum, people with whom I could get things off my chest. Finding yourself part of a group of supportive people who care and who can provide invaluable advice can really help to restore flagging spirits. It'll help you to muster your energy and confidence, to make you feel good about yourself again. Remember: when you are tired and doubting yourself, you simply won't be able to make the best possible decisions.

Despite always being in competition with other CEOs, your peers can also provide a support network. When you get together with other CEOs, you can learn from each other. You may feel like you are all alone running your company; being at the top can feel like a lonely sport when you're unsure who to trust and who to take advice from, or what their own self-interest is. But, after the points have been scored and tackles missed, when you come off the pitch those other CEOs are in a unique position to know how you feel. Shake hands and buy each other a beer.

Find a productive routine

Remember that Admiral and his daily 'Little Lie Down' routine we encountered in Chapter 3? Everyone has a different rhythm for optimal productivity, but here is a routine that worked for me and could potentially work for you, too. I used to wake up at 6.10 a.m. and read emails to check for potential issues. Then I read the local and *Financial Times* news websites. While I expected that nothing untoward would have occurred overnight, I knew that, if it had, I would be ahead of the game and able to contemplate appropriate responses and options before being exposed to the glare of the work environment.

I also recommend that you do at least 30 minutes of exercise each day. This becomes surprisingly easy when you are in a good routine; work on a plan to get into that habit. Getting a personal trainer or joining a class can help with motivation and ensure you're making the most of the limited time available to you.

Reconnecting with your family is also important. Inform them, without boring them to distraction, what you and the company are up to. Highlight the positives; your family are already burdened with your frequent absences and distraction at home, so they deserve to celebrate the wins.

Improve yourself – and everyone else

In their 2014 book, *How Google Works*,[1] ex-Google CEO, Eric Schmidt and his one-time colleague, Jonathan Rosenberg, shared

---

[1] E. Schmidt and J. Rosenberg, *How Google works*. John Murray, 2014.

that hiring and retaining the right talent is an absolute top priority at the company. The reason for this is that the company is powered by the people Schmidt and Rosenberg call 'smart creatives'. To attract this optimum kind of talent, they went on record as saying that they 'Hire them not for the knowledge they possess, but for the things they don't yet know.'

Staying curious, being agile and continuing to seek out and take opportunities to learn are crucial attributes for successful CEOs, both for themselves and for the cultures they instil at their organizations. If you don't continue to grow as a leader, then the entire organization is likely to be in that state as well. Modelling the right behaviours here really matters. Otherwise, there's a real danger that employees will think: 'Why should I develop myself, if my boss doesn't bother to do it?' Only by seeking constant improvement can you grow and continue to add value to yourself, your company and your community.

Make sure that you, and every member of the team, has a clearly defined set of improvement goals that they have agreed with their line leaders and management. Then give them the time and space to accomplish them.

I once worked at a major bank and we had a number of compulsory self-improvement courses which I took delight in not attending (including time management, which I failed and was sent back for retraining on). Noticing my poor attendance record, my boss pulled me aside.

'Don't be arrogant and think that all this is beneath you,' he said, waving off my protestations, 'where else are you going to get paid to learn, to develop, to improve? I don't care if the next course is in macramé; you are going!'

So I did. I've never taken my own development for granted ever since.

Making decisions

Accept that you aren't perfect

Everyone in a management or leadership role can find themselves in the 'squeezed middle'. Even as CEO, you are generally looked up to by your team and down on by your board, investors, media and, often, industry peers. This places in your own mind a huge pressure to always be right. It's important to recognize that's not possible.

Proving that you're a skilled decision-maker might have been one of the reasons you got your role in the first place. However, unlike decision-making in other roles, CEO decision-making is not always a matter of simply choosing to do the right thing, or effecting a compromise. The sheer volume of decisions to be made on a regular basis can be daunting. In many cases, you will only have imperfect or partial information; and, of course, a looming deadline.

You have two options:

1. Delay, obfuscate and seek to make the most perfect decision at a later date, by which time the issue will have changed, or the opportunity been lost.
2. Dig deep into your wells of experience and knowledge, add input from those equipped to give it, and make a decision.

You may have to accept that the choice you made, quite possibly, and with the benefit of hindsight, won't always have been for the best.

As we saw in Chapter 9, one of US General Colin Powell's leadership principles is about making those tricky judgement calls. He says that every time you face a tough choice, you should have no less than 40% and up to 70% of the information you need to make that decision. If you make a decision with less than 40% of the information you need, you are 'shooting from the hip' and will make too many mistakes.

It's the second part of this decision-making rule that surprises many leaders. They often think that they need more than 70% of the information before they can make a decision. But, if you wait until you're approaching 100% sure, the opportunity has usually passed and someone else will have beaten you to the punch.

According to leadership coach and author Dr Steven Anderson of Orange Dot Consulting:

> A key element that supports Powell's rule is the notion that intuition is what separates the great leaders from the average ones. Intuition is what allows us to make tough decisions well, but many of us ignore our gut. We want certainty that we are making the right decision, but that is not possible. In my experience, people who want certainty in their decisions end up working for other people, not leading.[2]

So, the next time you have a tough decision to make, do what Colin Powell does: get just enough information to make an informed decision and then trust your gut. Chronicle your decision-making process too; this will help explain it and enable you to learn from it, whether it was ultimately a good or bad call.

Unfortunately, perfection is hard to achieve on a daily basis. I'm not suggesting at all that you should not set a high standard or accept mediocrity, but setting too high a bar often results in delay and obfuscation, as the organization strives to produce the impossible.

Beware, too, of trying to take into account all the varied opinions of employees, investors, board members, well-wishers and those who have more nefarious reasons for providing opinions. Analysis paralysis is a real threat. When you are under fire, you have to

[2] S. L. Anderson, 'The 40-70 rule', Integrated Leadership Systems. Available from http://integratedleader.com/articles/40-70rule.pdf [accessed 18 August 2020].

move, trust your training and that of those around you. Sitting still is an option of limited appeal.

Admiral James Stavridis, a former Supreme Allied Commander, sums this up neatly:

> What a leader has to do is within yourself be free to make the kind of judgements, the kind of moral and ethical judgements, and not allow outsiders to impose that on you. Outside influences... as leaders we are becoming excessively attuned to those and we are underweight following that internal moral compass.[3]

Trusting your gut

When you don't trust your gut and override that 'this doesn't feel right' sensation, you are giving up millions of years of survival evolution, even if you can't put your finger on why. Many years ago, I was lectured on this topic by an old, highly decorated 'spook' who told the story of calling off a raid on the house of a known terrorist. All he had to do that night was drive past the house and confirm the target was home. Once he had given the signal, all hell was to break loose with special forces troops descending from choppers and securing the area, while ground troops massed on the street to provide cover and effect the arrest. As he drove down the street, he felt that something wasn't right. After wrestling with his duty and the feeling of unease he called the operation off, resulting in a career-threatening exchange with his Commanding Officer.

---

[3] CNBC, 'How to future-proof companies and CEOs: Highlights from CNBC Evolve', *CNBC*. Available from www.cnbc.com/2019/06/21/how-to-future-proof-companies-and-ceos-highlights-from-cnbc-evolve.html [accessed 18 August 2020].

Later, it emerged that there had been a leak and the area was ringed with explosives primed to go off as the force arrived. His only response when asked later how he had known was 'The kids weren't playing in the street.' His conscious self may not have picked up on the danger but his 'gut' had.

Keeping your finger on the pulse

We've already seen that while there is a veritable firehose of information trained on the CEO, much of it is biased, partial, self-serving, inaccurate or just wrong. Those trying to curry favour are to be watched as closely as those working their own agendas; they may be equally disruptive and as negative an influence on the good order of any organization.

That's why it's such a difficult challenge to source regular, reliable sources of information without bypassing organizational structures, appearing to play favourites or casting the information providers as potential informers and making them pariahs with their own teams. Here are some ideas for keeping your finger on the pulse without frightening the horses.

Try group information gathering

Events such as 'brown bag' lunches (or a variant thereof) can be a great way of facilitating two-way information exchange and learning. Regular sessions with trusted heads of departments and face-to-face communications with internal and external influencers can also be a great way of keeping in touch.

Go walkabout

MBWA – management by walking around – is not as daft a suggestion as it sounds. A CEO walkabout is important not just for showing your face and getting a sense of morale outside HQ or the C-suite; it's also great for picking up the tidbits of information which invariably emerge from exchanges with team members, however brief.

Cultivate your friends on the board

Without appearing Machiavellian, it may also be useful to cultivate members of the board with whom you have a good relationship. This will allow you to test the temperature and open exchanges of views on the direction of the company outside more formal lines of communication. In this, the importance of an open and transparent relationship with your Chair cannot be over emphasized.

Look outside

Find external advisors, trusted (often paid) professionals who, unshackled from corporate politics by the contractual nature of their appointments, can provide support in various areas of operations. These are the people who will give you unvarnished feedback and challenge your thinking in an open and honest way. Seek out their input and insights. External consultants can also act as a circuit breaker to help bring about organizational change and efficiencies if they are properly managed and on message.

A word of warning, though; don't get into a situation where they exert (or appear to exert) too much influence over operations, as team members might feel threatened or undermined by them. A conversation which ends up with 'I work for you, not them' can be a slippery slope.

Managing your time

The research by Michael Porter and Nitin Nohria into how CEOs spend their time that we looked at in Chapter 1 is unequivocal: 'the way CEOs allocate their time and their presence – where they choose to personally participate – is crucial, not only to their own

effectiveness but also to the performance of their companies.'4
How and where a CEO spends time not only determines what
gets done, but also signals priorities for others. Stay too remote
and you're in danger of seeming distant and out of touch; spend
too much time on direct decision-making and you'll seem like a
micro-manager.

Interestingly, the CEOs who took part in Porter and Nohria's
research allocated their time quite differently. Some of this they
accounted for by sectoral and cultural differences which are hard
to control, but more discretionary things like participation in
company rituals that offered limited return or a CEO's own habits
also played a part. It seems that there are definitely things CEOs
can do to improve their time management. That's what we'll be
looking at in the rest of this chapter.

I was fortunate to have had the President of Blackstone, Tony
James, as one of my mentors. While travelling with him in the
Asia Pacific, I noticed that he would receive anything between six
and 700 emails a day, on the other side of the world to his office.
But by the end of each day, he had cleared the majority of these...
only for his inbox to fill up again by the next day. Sound familiar?

I asked him how he dealt with this inundation and he replied:

> It's like peeling an onion; you scan for the most important
> people or topics, or those marked 'Urgent, please read!',
> then you look for the subject and people you want to hear
> about or from, so by the time you have finished going
> through those, you are into a rhythm and the onion gets
> smaller.

This is at the crux of time management as a CEO. You need to
develop an understanding of what issues you need to deal with

4 M. Porter and N. Nohria, 'How CEOs manage time', *Harvard Business Review*, July–August 2018. Available from https://hbr.org/2018/07/the-leaders-calendar [accessed 18 August 2020].

immediately, what can be deferred and what can be delegated. As one respondent in the Egon Zehnder 2018 survey noted: 'If the "doing" doesn't lead to "being", then delegate.'

When I first became CEO, I had created the tone of being the 'everywhere CEO' – always approachable and available. That was an error. I ended up being stretched in multiple directions and upsetting a lot of people in the process, including myself. You need to accept that there simply isn't enough of you to go around, and manage your time accordingly.

How to deal with the feeling of being overwhelmed

Early on in my Navy training I was appointed Officer of the Day. I had to get my fellow trainees to our scheduled sessions, take charge of the parade formations and take responsibility for the welfare of my team. I was feeling the pressure, issuing incorrect orders and thinking I was doing a terrible job. The Drill Petty Officer, whose job it was to mould us into some semblance of an Officer Corps, took me aside and said: 'Sir, you are doing good. Don't sweat the small stuff. And remember, Sir… it's all small stuff!'

In my CEO roles, I quickly realized I didn't need to be dealing with the little things. I couldn't add value to them and shouldn't have been giving time to them. Every time someone tried to pass me something to do that could be delegated, I assigned it to someone else that was better equipped to deal with it. I quickly learnt that my role was to ensure the entire organization ran smoothly, not to do everyone's job.

Pick your battles and the battleground

A huge lesson I learnt is that you don't need to be right all the time. That may seem counter-intuitive, but it's important to recognize. Let situations play out without calling them early. You might end up being wrong, but if you wait and observe and are ultimately right, the outcome will emerge as you have predicted and planned for, without you being seen as having forced it.

The same is true of battles. There are some that aren't worth winning – they risk too much collateral damage and residual resentment. Others are not worth the energy that would need to be expended to secure a minor win or minimal impact. Calculate the return on investment for using your valuable time; it's a scarce resource.

Impose discipline – but be flexible

Managing your time requires a very strict discipline. However, you need to keep free time in your diary for the unexpected. For example, if you get a phone call from someone who says there has been unusual trading in your stock, no matter what you had planned to do originally, you now need to deal with that issue for the rest of the day. Have a plan for the day but also recognize the plan will get chopped to pieces by the end of it.

I was getting frustrated because people were slotting things into my diary. I was late for meetings I didn't know existed. Eventually, I said: 'Nobody touches my diary except my PA, and her job is to gatekeep my appointments.' I was not being arrogant; I was just trying to remain sane.

I matured as a leader when I found out things weren't being done. At the end of every quarter, I would get the financials for that period and spend two days analysing them to work out what was happening. I used to hate it if the CFO said: 'I'll get back to you, my team has let me down.' At that point, I would say: 'You need to be doing your job – running your team and getting them to provide you with the answers – so I can do mine. And don't blame your team in front of me; you are responsible for them.'

Prioritize

It almost goes without saying that you need to prioritize. False priorities will crop up in your calendar and end up driving you mad. You need to be firm, while remaining sensitive to cultural and personal constraints.

I was sitting at my desk dealing with a myriad of issues when the Head of HR came to me and said: 'I need your help to decide on the design of the Hongbao.' In Chinese societies, the Hongbao is a red envelope filled with money that you give to staff and their families, as well as people you do business with, on Chinese New Year or special occasions like a wedding. It is taken very seriously and the envelopes are very ornate. Given all that I had on my plate at that time, my response was: 'I trust you. You run the Hongbao design and I'll run the company.' But a note of caution: saying 'no' arbitrarily may be dangerous because you can seem insensitive and you may breach cultural sensitivities.

List five to ten things to be done for the day, and order them based on complexity and urgency. If my day went according to plan, I would get all my tasks done. If something went over time, I would prioritize accordingly. If I could get results doing a 'quick and dirty' job, I would, or else I'd aim to delegate, to ensure that I could get back to my main task – running the company. Sometimes it took me a week to go through four key things. You have got to keep re-prioritizing, based on importance and urgency, until you achieve the objectives desired.

The key question to ask yourself at all times is: 'Am I adding value here?' Ask it of yourself several times a day. If you can and are, great. If not, delegate, but remember to track some of the issues that have been delegated to ensure that they are actually getting done.

Create blocks of time with gaps in between

Every day, make sure that you create blocks of time for specific activities to give your day structure. Schedule them around your own rhythms, so important decisions are taken when you are at your best and more routine matters dealt with at your low-energy points.

Make sure there are gaps of free time in between each block of scheduled time, when you can deal with phone calls and emails, or any unforeseen things that crop up, such as a compliance or an HR issue. Recognize that sometimes the person who plans your diary doesn't realize that sometimes you end up running around like a lunatic, as they haven't factored the time you need to get from one meeting to the next into your schedule. You need to communicate your needs to them.

I used to sit down with my PA on Monday morning to go through the week's diary. I would always look for potential diary clashes, unrealistic timings or anything that could be reassigned. For everything left, I became very strict with the timeframes allocated.

Be very strict with your time

Assign half an hour, maximum, for meetings, and insist there is an agenda. At the start of every meeting, make it clear that: 'We have 30 minutes. That's the agenda. Let's go.' If the meeting needs to continue, you could assign someone else to take over from that point or, once you have identified what needs to be done, tell them, and then delegate that action to someone who will then be accountable for it.

Some people may feel you are abrupt or that they have been shortchanged, but they'll get used to it. Most meetings are too long, unfocused and unproductive; this approach doesn't only make better use of your own time; it also values the time of everyone else who attends, freeing them up to do their own jobs. It may sound brutal but, if you let them, people will take up time to get reassurance, feel better, prove their worth or tell you how fantastic they are. You – and all of your colleagues – have better things to do with your time.

12

Crisis Management

'Never let a good crisis go to waste.'

Rahm Emanuel,
Barack Obama's Chief of Staff

I WAS INCREDIBLY fortunate to have competed in the 75th Rolex Sydney to Hobart Yacht Race. The job of our skipper, ex-Royal Air Force Officer and Round the World sailor, Marcus Cholerton-Brown, was to take a ragtag bunch of sailors, most of whom had never sailed together before, and turn us into a safe, cohesive team with a chance of winning our Division. He prepared us for the unexpected changes in the weather, sail condition and sea state. He constantly asked: 'What's the plan if this sail blows or the wind picks up, or drops? Think ahead. Have another sail ready.' He encouraged us to be alert and always to think about what might happen next. So, when five hours into the race, our bowsprit blew off, taking our spinnaker with it, we swung into coordinated action, repaired the damage and safely completed the race.

We saw in Chapter 1 that, of the CEOs interviewed by Michael Porter and Nitin Nohria for their research into how CEOs spend their time, most of them had to deal with a full-blown crisis. It's the CEO's job to expect the unexpected and to deal with it. Sooner or later, you'll be facing your own damaged bowsprit and spinnaker, one of Donald Rumsfeld's 'unknown unknowns'. You'll need to be ready.

Random regulatory audits; hostile takeover bids; unexpected questions at an investor presentation; someone falling off a roof… just a few of the travails sent to try any CEO. When the worst happens, you need to remember that you are the public and the private face of the company. You need to come up with urgent solutions for unexpected situations, to communicate the issues you are facing and what you are going to do as a result. Unless you are prepared, with properly trained staff, it's easy, in times like these, to spiral out of control.

Crisis action planning

If you don't have a crisis action plan, then you are going to be in a world of pain. Get one. To use a military maxim, adopt the 6Ps: Perfect Preparation Prevents Piss Poor Performance.

The unexpected requires as much planning, if not more, than the normal course of business. Plan for it, be creative in your scenario planning; business continuity planning (BCP) is often a fundamental regulatory requirement as well as being good practice. You can't afford to ignore it and you will be assessed on its effectiveness.

All staff need to know what action needs to be taken when 'shit happens'. By having a plan, something to fall back on when a crisis occurs, you will have a starting point for recovery. Make sure that everyone knows what their roles and responsibilities will be and that they have cascaded the relevant information down to their teams:

- Who has responsibility for the initial response?
- Who puts together a team to deal with the issue?
- Who reports to the board and who decides when to go public with the issue, with what message?

And crucially:

- How do you learn from the issue and ensure that it doesn't happen again?

Never let a good crisis go to waste.

Make sure you involve your board in the planning. There should be no surprises for them; they should know what you propose to do in any number of situations and are prepared for it. Your external advisors should be similarly briefed and know what you expect from them.

Having a team ready to deal with the barrage of issues that all companies face regularly, and being able to prioritize which are the most impactful or even existential, is a key goal for any CEO.

Practise crisis management

Don't wait until the worst happens. Put in place multiple scenarios and practise them. Train and develop your people so that, when bad things happen, everybody knows what to do. In Naval operations, particularly at sea, multiple scenarios are practised all the time: 'man overboard'; 'missiles inbound'; 'brace, brace, brace – collision imminent' – it doesn't matter what the call is, the whole ship moves to action the plan immediately and effectively as the crew knows exactly what they are expected to do. Post-mortems are carried out to find where things were not done as they should have been, the learnings noted and are expected to be actioned next time, because 'Next time Sir, it might be the real thing and we can't wait for you to finish your cup of tea!!'

During my first CEO tenure, the company was potentially vulnerable to a hostile takeover. In preparation for this eventuality we devised 'Project Citadel'. The plan would be activated by me sending out an email convening a Project Citadel meeting advising that we had received a hostile bid. At that stage, all staff involved would forget what they were currently working on and activate their part of the plan, not knowing whether it was real or not. For example, I would take the lead on communication to avoid panic, maintain an overall view of the situation, issue instructions and keep all relevant stakeholders informed, including our lawyers and investment banks. I would then inform the board and launch a takeover defence.

When the bid was finally lobbed at us, the plan swung into action and the takeover was politely but forcefully rebuffed. If you're practised enough, when a crisis does hit, you'll be better prepared to take charge, take responsibility and execute your plan, adjusting where necessary to deal with the vagaries of the situation you are faced with.

And don't become complacent. Once complacency sets in, it pervades the organization and degrades not only performance but resilience to shocks – be they internal or external.

The ready-for-anything plan

My mentor, John Connolly, is known internationally for his skills in crisis management. Preparation should probably be his middle name.

Before AGMs or face-to-face presentations by analysts, John would set up question-and-answer sessions where he pummelled us with difficult, abrasive questions such as: 'Question for the CEO – the share price has gone down 20% and your pay packet has gone up 35%; how do you justify it?' John would tear apart our responses and body language, telling us that we looked defensive or grumpy; we needed to take a deep breath; we should answer the question respectfully, reframe it, use your training, don't react and make sure you don't get yourself into trouble.

In the majority of cases, by the time we finished the meeting or AGM, we would look at the audience and think: 'Is that really the best you've got?' This was no accident: we were so well prepared because we had to be. Anything else would have been tantamount to treating the company and our shareholders with disrespect, something that erodes goodwill and ultimately leads to an epic fall from grace.

It was a lesson in planning for the unknown unknowns that has served me well.

Leadership in times of high uncertainty

Many crises seem acute when they're happening but can be resolved within a specific timeframe.

A report written by Korn Ferry during the global Covid-19 pandemic in 2020 offers excellent advice for how leaders can react when those timeframes are more uncertain.[1] It's also not a bad blueprint for crisis management more generally.

The report is clear that high levels of uncertainty need agile, adaptive leaders to step up and take charge. In times of crisis, people depend on leaders to provide clarity and hope. Fear can be contagious, breeding irrational behaviour and anxiety, which is fatal to the good order of the organization and its ultimate survival. It's a time to make the most of the emotional intelligence we talked about in Chapter 2: you'll need to be self-aware and self-controlled; show empathy; coach and inspire. This is a time for both 'being' and 'doing'. The following is quoted from the report:

---

[1] Korn Ferry, *Managing through crisis and preparing for the post-outbreak era: A leader's playbook for a year of two halves.* Available from https://focus.kornferry.com/wp-content/uploads/2015/02/KornFerry-A-Leaders-Playbook-for-a-Year-of-Two-Halves.pdf [accessed 18 August 2020].

BE

Calm

Control your emotions. Stress and negativity can be contagious, and can shut down your neocortex – and with it your ability to reason and problem-solve.

Confident & positive

You are highly skilled; no one understands your business and context better. Your instincts are often the best judgement.

Courageous

Be willing to launch without guarantee of success. Endure – as a leader you have to hold steady, persevere and persist.

Empathetic

Show people you care and understand their situation. Know where your people are in the grief curve.

Resilient

Be an energy bringer. Practice 'Creative Abandonment'; ignore what drains your time and resources and concentrate on the must wins.

DO

Express a vision

It is everyone's 'north star'. It guides and motivates and you cannot 'overdo' it.

Communicate a lot, authentically

The only thing faster than the speed of light are rumours. Tell the real and informed story of what's happening.

Act!

In difficulty, always default to a bias to action: Decide – Accept – Feedback – Self correct.

Seek clarity

Face the world as it is and not how you wish it to be, even on unpopular topics and thorny issues.

Keep it simple and purposeful

Remind people what's really important – common goals, clearly understood. Practice ruthless prioritisation on your main goal.

It's also important to be authentic and humble. In such times of uncertainty and ambiguity, it's more than ever acceptable not to have all the answers. Listen to employee concerns and acknowledge there are sometimes no easy solutions. If you don't have the answer, bring your team together to discuss and experiment with solutions – focus on testing new things quickly. Being transparent and open in this way can go a long way to building credibility and trust with staff, customers, shareholders and the wider community.

If you have to make tough decisions about redundancies or forced leave, be clear and upfront about your plan. Do it once and move forward. Don't fall into the trap of the COO of a major global bank sent from HQ to Asia to sack the much-loved Asia CEO and close multiple departments. He called a town hall meeting and announced: 'OK, Team! It's business as usual... until it isn't.' Nice! The word most often used to describe him afterwards rhymed with 'banker'. His approach formed the basis of my lifelong aversion to the phrase 'business as usual' in unusual situations.

And, even in the most difficult crisis, make sure you look after your team as well as possible. Be generous with recognition and continue to offer opportunities for professional development. You're going to need your key players when the crisis is over.

13

Governance, Compliance and Risk

'Tempting as it might be, never rely on the "eleventh" commandment: don't get caught. Do the right thing.'

Anonymous

FROM PONZI SCHEMES to the collapse of Lehman Brothers; dodgy accounting practices at Enron to any number of boardroom failures revealed in the wake of the 2008 financial crisis, it's clear that plenty of business leaders have been prepared to bend the rules when it comes to running their organizations. On balance, though, relying on the 'eleventh commandment' – don't get caught – might not be the wisest leadership strategy.

For some, the inherently back-office world of governance, risk and compliance (GRC) can sound, well, a bit dull. It's the kind of work that very rarely gets praised or sometimes even noticed. But here's the thing: getting it right is not only a matter of good practice; it's what stands between you, a hefty fine or even a jail sentence, trashing your reputation, not to mention that of your board and the company, in the process.

That's why it's so important to instil positive cultures around compliance and governance in your organization and to make it your responsibility – as CEO – to make sure everyone buys into it. It may sound tempting to take shortcuts or to ignore yet another set of regulations, but the rules are the rules. You might as well get on board with them. Better still, make compliance one of your core values.

Governance, risk and compliance: Some definitions

Governance is the effective, ethical management of a company by its senior executives (including non-executive board members) and managers.

Risk is the ability to mitigate risks that can hinder an organization's operations or ability to remain competitive in its market.

Compliance is a company's adherence to regulatory requirements for business operations and other practices.

Compliance can be a tricky business, especially if you're operating in a highly regulated sector, such as financial services, or across jurisdictions. That's why it's important to ensure you know what the rules are, and to have the processes and people in place to keep on top of new or amended regulations and governance best practice.

Be prepared

There are a number of ways in which you can prepare yourself for the governance and compliance challenge.

Get formal training around your responsibilities

I attended a Company Directors' Course at the Australian Institute of Company Directors, which gave me formal training about the roles, responsibilities and liabilities of a board director, and the CEO in particular. It gave me a vital underpinning and helped me to know what was expected of me; the right board protocols and practices, and how to interpret and analyse financial reports and all of the other strategic and operation information that make up an average board meeting agenda. Remember that as a company director you are deemed to have knowledge of the issues contained in board papers. With your Chair, the CEO is ultimately responsible for setting the tone of the company and its activities. Make sure you're prepared for what that really means.

Understand the rules around your products and markets

Make sure you and your team keep abreast of what's going on in relation to your products and markets. Whenever you can, attend industry conferences and presentations. Ask your lawyers and accountants to conduct in-house training on key issues and areas of importance. Involving your senior team is a great way to make sure everyone commits to ongoing self-improvement, which is so vital in any environment.

Keep compliant

Laws and regulations are not static things; they change – more often than you might think. Make sure you stay on top of your own specific regulatory environment, and that you're up to speed and compliant with anything new. If you aren't, identify what you need to do to ensure you are meeting the requirements of the regulators. Don't treat regulators with contempt; engage with them and establish trust.

Mind the people stuff

Wherever you operate, provided that you employ people, you will always need to pay attention to the details of employment, and health and safety regulations. This is serious stuff, and you may be criminally liable if your people aren't employed on a proper basis or briefed, trained and safely equipped. You need a safety culture in your organization; make sure the workplace is safe and conducive to harmonious interaction between all employees.

I can't emphasize enough how important all these steps are. You have a legal liability, a formal duty of care, to do the right thing. It's not a light-hearted role and people – including your investors and stakeholders – are affected by your decisions. If you don't have a safety culture within your business, people will get hurt.

A GRC checklist

This is not the place for a completely comprehensive compliance checklist, but you might want to consider the following as a starting point:

✓ Policies and procedures: what do you need and do you have them? Are they up to date and does every employee know what they are, and what is expected of them? Has each employee confirmed that they have reviewed the procedures relevant to them, in writing?

✓ Regulatory compliance: are all forms lodged in an accurate and timely way? Is there a filing schedule in place to ensure that late filings are avoided?

✓ Training: are all staff trained as required? Is there an ongoing training plan to make sure training is topped up as necessary?

✓ Are all necessary checks (for example, for Anti-Money Laundering [AML]) complete and up to date?

✓ Business continuity planning (BCP): is there a BCP in place and has it been practised recently?

✓ Board meetings, agendas and minutes: is there a schedule of meetings that has been agreed with the board? Are board agendas, minutes and resolutions properly constituted, logged and stored?

✓ Internal audit: has the latest report been presented and the issues raised in it addressed?

✓ Risk management: do you have an up-to-date risk register, identifying a hierarchy of risks, their likelihood and mitigation strategies, with a clear plan for dealing with those that are of concern?

✓ What have you missed? Keep asking this question; it might keep you out of jail.

Extract from a typical compliance section of a set of board papers

Compliance

2.1. Policy on Management of Legal Matters – in progress, to be completed by end of the month

2.2. AML Remediation – on track (completion end of March)

2.3. To draft vendor selection template for all to use – in progress, to be completed by end of the month

2.4. Board Schedule – to check if BOD and ARCC can be re-scheduled, as requested

2.5. Board Committees – to approve the committees' terms of reference

Working with the board

Some newly minted CEOs might incorrectly assume that, having reached the top of the pile, they are the ultimate authority. Wrong. While you are certainly responsible for everything that happens in the company (whether you had anything to do with it or not!), the reality is that you're simply swapping an individual boss for a whole group of individuals: your board.

It's the board that hires you, and the board who can fire you. Board members will evaluate your performance and set your compensation. They have the power to approve strategies and budgets, new investments and moves into other markets/product lines. In some cases, they might even have the right to approve or veto over key hires and investor outreach. Bear in mind, too, that every board will include a mix of personalities who bring with them their own attitudes, prejudices, preferences and foibles.

It's a situation rife with potential for misunderstandings, misinterpretations and conflict. It's up to you, as CEO, together with your Chair, to make sure the board functions and contributes as effectively as possible. Don't try to 'manage' them, or keep them at arm's length. The best board relationships are based on trust, openness and a willingness for executives and non-executives to work in partnership. If, as CEO, you're open and collaborative, you'll be able to build mutual respect and support. While the board might not always be supportive of everything you want to do, it needs to know that you are coming from a sense of 'doing the right thing' in all of your decisions and trust you to do that. You really are all in it together.

John Poynton is clear that the key relationship is between the CEO and the Chair. When things go well, the Chair can be an invaluable guide and mentor, supporting the CEO through all sorts of thorny issues like corporate culture and board relations. He or she can also act as an advocate for the CEO, both internally and externally. A good symbiotic relationship adds significantly to the experiences of both, to the benefit of all stakeholders. If, however, there's a lack of respect and trust, and communication breaks down, the value of the company is seriously under threat. Where the relationship has broken down to the extent that the board is not functioning properly, the most likely outcome is the departure of one or other of the protagonists. Often – and sometimes unfairly – this will be the CEO. It's a lesson worth learning.

It's also essential that boards are properly constituted, with a variety of knowledge bases and experiences. The best boards are also willing to debate the established norms and challenge entrenched ways of doing things. Despite the fact that many boards comprise like-minded individuals, mostly men, with similar experience sets, there are real – and proven – benefits of more diverse boards, whether in terms of demographics, life experience or approach. You would do well to make board diversity a priority for you and your Chair.

What a Chair looks for in a CEO

John Poynton has identified some key common characteristics of successful CEOs:

A willingness to listen

No one has all the answers all the time. The best CEOs surround themselves with subject matter experts and smart people, and are prepared to take their advice.

Lack of hubris

They lead by example and take responsibility but will also portray themselves as humble, willing to take on board differing views and demonstrate high EQ at all times.

Curiosity

They exhibit intellectual curiosity about the world around them, as well as their own industry and the role it plays in wider society.

Outside-the-box thinking

They are willing to think outside the box, to 'have a crack', and have a track record for doing so previously, with some degree of success.

Stakeholder alignment

They take stakeholders on a journey, communicating strategy and progress towards identified goals and making sure that everyone is aligned and informed.

Top tips for working with your board

Establish trust and respect early on

Make sure your communication with the board is respectful, honest, open and genuine. Most board members will inevitably know less about the company, or even your industry, but never let the board feel that you as CEO are disrespecting them.

Regulate the amount of information the board receives

Find out how they'd like board papers to be presented, what information they would like to see, and in what format. I was once (rightly) admonished by a board Chair, who said:

> You have just presented over 400 pages of board papers. Under the law I am deemed to have read them, so I have to. So give me the information I need in a summary form and keep the rest to management reports, available to me and the rest of the board if we need them. Otherwise, we might think that you are trying to hide something in a mountain of bullshit.

Provide regular updates

Don't always wait for set-piece board meetings, or always treat board members as a group. Provide informal updates and meet with board members individually too.

Operate a 'no-surprises culture'

Keep them informed, involve them in critical paths to decision-making and never, ever surprise them. Transparency is your friend.

Set the tone

Inform them of the good news fast – but tell them the bad news faster.

Take a health check on the board's perception of you

On a regular basis, consult with the Chair and other directors with whom you have built a level of trust and mutual respect. Get them to unofficially critique your performance and provide constructive criticism.

Keep your word

Always do what you say you are going to do.

Working with investors

You'll also need to work on your relationship with another key group of stakeholders: your investors. It's important to achieve a balance here. On the one hand, good governance suggests an open, transparent relationship with plenty of communication and opportunities for information exchange. But remember those seven new CEO surprises reported in the *Harvard Business Review* and outlined in the Introduction? Surprise #6 suggests that *Pleasing Shareholders Is Not the Goal.*

The fact is that many shareholders hold stock for a very short time indeed. That means that, in many cases, their interests are not naturally aligned with your longer-term CEO vision for your company. There is a huge disconnect between quarterly performance and long-term strategy. If you fall into the trap, and it's easy to do so, of concentrating all your efforts on the company's quarterly performance, then the long-term strategy will be for someone else to worry about because, at some point, your quarterly performance will fail, you'll get axed and the next person will be in the hot seat!

Perhaps it's not surprising that one CEO interviewed for the HBR study went on record as saying: 'There comes a time, when you just don't give a damn what the analysts think!'[1] The bottom line is that CEOs need to concern themselves with creating sustainable economic value. What you need to do is to persuade the analysts that there is sufficient quarterly performance to keep them happy and interested – while at the same time adhering to your longer-term plan to future-proof the business.

For example, in the real estate world, capex is the money you allocate to maintaining your assets, basically repairs and maintenance. You can make yourself look very clever for a couple of years by not spending a cent on your buildings, so your distribution is always going up and there is free cash flow to pay down debt. You may look fantastic; you may have no costs. But, meanwhile, the buildings are falling apart and at some point (and you pray it's not on your watch) the roof is going to fall in.

---

[1] M. E. Porter, J. W. Lorsch and N. Nohria, 'Seven surprises for new CEOs', *Harvard Business Review*, October 2004. Available from https://hbr.org/2004/10/seven-surprises-for-new-ceos [accessed 18 August 2020].

Top tips for investor relations

Be as open and transparent as you can be
But bear in mind any restrictions within a regulated environment.

Be clear and responsive
Be seen as the leader of an organization that does the right thing and answers questions.

Give regular updates
Tell investors what you've done and what you'll do next.

Build trust
Become the considered face of the company. Treat all investors with equanimity; approach them with respect; answer their questions fully. Don't obfuscate, and don't surprise them, either.

Be prepared
Make sure you have the right disaster recovery crisis action plans in place.

Understand materiality
If you are operating under a regulatory regime that requires continuous disclosure, understand the concept of materiality and ensure the disclosures from the company and the public are vetted and signed off.

Environmental, social and governance criteria

ESG (environmental, social and governance) criteria have become critical in the day-to-day operations for companies big and small.

Unlike CSR (corporate social responsibility), often considered its forerunner and a form of self-regulation around a company's efforts to have a positive impact on its employees, consumers, the environment and wider community, ESG takes this a step further by *measuring* these activities to arrive at a more precise assessment of a company's actions.

In particular, ESG looks at how businesses:

- respond to climate change;
- treat their workers;
- build trust and foster innovation;
- manage their supply chains.

Rather than simply relying on grand CSR statements, ESG demands metrics, whether in amounts of energy saved, emissions traded or water preserved.

ESG activity is seen as vital to corporate purpose, strategy and company governance. It's a key assessment marker for investors, so it's important to be able to demonstrate your ESG credentials. Ideally, it needs to be fully embedded in your operations.

I've always been keen to take ESG seriously. A decade ago, however, it was not a view shared by my board, who saw being more environmentally aware as a cost rather than an opportunity. But I remained determined to lessen our energy footprint, and I was convinced it would lead to cost savings too. I convinced my management team that, located in the tropics as we were, we were ideally placed to take advantage of solar power. We had over 50 properties with flat roofs. Fitting solar panels felt like a win-win-win for our tenants, our shareholders and the company. And we'd also get to be good corporate citizens.

Despite the team's reluctance, for once, I pulled rank. We assembled a working group and got creative, using a scheme called solar lease, whereby the solar panel provider could lease the roof from us in return for a rebate on our electricity costs, with any surplus power given to the providers to sell. A year later, we had solar panels on 29 roofs, and we were nominated for an award as the greatest contributor to solar power on the island.

Standing at the dais on the awards night and receiving the award was very satisfying but, more importantly, it showed what can be done when you combine a constructively creative solution with good communication and a desire to do the right thing. Our achievement also encouraged others in our industry to follow suit, increasing the number of solar panels on commercial roofs significantly.

This is business. You need to be able to face the approbation of shareholders, the board, the community and staff, but be humble and recognize that you are not always going to be right. As long as you keep doing the right thing, you are going to be OK. Remember these wise words from headhunter Tahnoon Pasha: 'the CEO has a duty of care to all stakeholders, often legally required but always a moral imperative. It is important to recognize that we can make a significant social impact without a detrimental impact on performance.'

Part 4

Peak #3: Leaving the business

14

Future-Proofing the Business

'Begin with the end in mind.'

Stephen R. Covey,
The 7 Habits of Highly Effective People

ONE OF STEPHEN Covey's seven habits might have been written especially for a CEO. As we've seen, the average tenure for a CEO tends to hover at or below five years. Thinking ahead, looking to future-proof the business and anticipating your own departure means that you will always need to *begin with the end in mind*. We'll look at the more personal aspects of having a good departure in Chapter 15; here we'll be focusing on the business you'll be leaving behind – how to create a lasting legacy you can look back on with satisfaction and pride.

It's almost beyond cliché to say that we live at a time of unprecedented change but, with the Fourth Industrial Revolution well underway, it's simply a fact of life for businesses and their CEOs. Once-proud brands, like Kodak and Boeing, or even the average newspaper, have had to face up to seismic changes to their markets, operations and customer bases. This presents special challenges for CEOs, who have a responsibility for leading organizations that are flexible, dynamic and adaptable in the face of change – while also keeping the day-to-day business running.

It's the classic balance explored by Clayton Christensen in his book *The Innovator's Dilemma*.[1] For Christensen, current business strengths can, in and of themselves, get in the way of innovation:

> …the decision-making and resource allocation processes that are key to the success of established companies are the very processes that reject disruptive technologies… These are the reasons why great firms stumbled or failed when confronted with disruptive technology change.

In a 2004 *Harvard Business Review* article, Charles A. O'Reilly and Michael L. Tushman also looked at the challenge leaders face when having to look both ways, keeping the business running while also anticipating and preparing their organizations for changes that will define the future. They introduce the concept of the 'ambidextrous' organization,[2] capable both of 'exploiting the present and exploring the future'. Their research shows that, when it came to innovation, the key to success is ambidextrous senior teams and managers able to lead across organizations, 'combining the attributes of rigorous cost cutters and free-thinking entrepreneurs'. Unsurprisingly, it's not easy. It requires complete buy-in at the top, absolute clarity of vision and purpose and regular communication at all levels of the business.

The age of agile

Back in 2001, 17 top software practitioners spent a long weekend at a US ski resort to discuss what constituted best practice for software development. The result was the

---

[1] C. M. Christensen, *The innovator's dilemma: When new technologies cause great firms to fail*. Harvard Business Review Press, 2016.

[2] C. A. O'Reilly III and M. L. Tushman, 'The ambidextrous organization', *The Harvard Business Review*, April 2004. Available from https://hbr.org/2004/04/the-ambidextrous-organization [accessed 18 August 2020].

Agile Manifesto,[3] a set of principles which summarize what has become a blueprint for agile, iterative, small-team and customer-facing project management.

Since then, commentators and researchers have been asking whether these techniques can be adapted and used in business more generally, especially at a time when traditional hierarchies and bureaucracies can seem at odds with a business landscape dominated by more fleet-of-foot tech giants like Amazon and Google.

Stephen Denning, author of the book *The Age of Agile*,[4] is firmly in the camp that sees agile management – or at least agile leadership mindsets – as the way forward. For Denning, there are three important characteristics:

1. Using small-team working to work on small tasks in short, iterative work cycles

2. A relentless focus on adding value for customers

3. The importance of coordinated work across cross-functional networks

Hybrid approaches, akin to O'Reilly and Tushman's 'ambidextrous' organization, are also under discussion. A 2018 report from the McKinsey Agile Tribe[5] charts the move away from what it calls organizations as *machines* (hierarchical and specialized) to organizations as *organisms* that combine

---

[3] *Manifesto for Agile Software Development*. Available from https:// agilemanifesto.org/ [accessed 18 August 2020].

[4] S. Denning, *The Age of Agile: How smart companies are transforming the way work gets done*. American Management Association, 2018.

[5] W. Aghina, K. Ahlback, A. De Smet, G. Lackey, M. Lurie, M. Murarka and C. Handscomb, 'The five trademarks of agile organizations', McKinsey & Company. Available from www.mckinsey.com/business-functions/organization/our-insights/the-five-trademarks-of-agile-organizations [accessed 18 August 2020].

'stable backbone elements that evolve slowly and support dynamic capabilities that can adapt quickly to new challenges and opportunities'.

It's an interesting debate – and certainly one worth considering when considering the future of your organization.

So just how can CEOs future-proof their organizations? My own experience suggests some key CEO tactics.

Be curious

Intellectual curiosity counts for a lot. Build and use your professional network to stay on top of industry trends. Watch the market and your competitors closely. Read widely. Keeping your finger on the pulse is one of your key roles as CEO.

Keep on top of the tech

Be on the lookout for the impact of technology – for both good and ill. This isn't just about implementing new software systems or digital marketing. It touches everything, including large-scale changes to market dynamics, like changing customer preferences and expectations. Think Uber and Airbnb, and the large-scale disruption their tech-enabled solutions have caused to long-established business models.

Look out for the game-changers

In the real estate space, the rise in demand for flexible workspace has been a game-changer for the industry. It's always difficult to separate a trend from a fad. Sometimes it's best to hold the line; other times – like the time I fought for overseas expansion (see Chapter 10) – you have to be brave and take a calculated risk.

You may not have the answers

Accept that, as is routine for a CEO, you may not have all the information to hand to make a perfect decision, but you will have to act decisively, so consider Colin Powell's 40/70 principle (see Chapter 9). We live in a world of uncertainty, whether that's continuing technological evolution, a global pandemic or the threat of climate change, and being able to live with and manage that uncertainty is crucial.

Hire in the right people with the right skills

To meet these challenges, you need, more than ever, the right people with the right skills doing the right things – and with the right mindsets. This goes for all levels – from the senior management team down to your apprentices. Enable your talent acquisition teams to adapt to new workplace dynamics like an increasingly contingent workforce and, more than ever, learning cultures will be essential.

Beware the risks

Looking to the future will always involve an element of risk. Some of these are known knowns – like the risk of cyber security or geopolitical instability – for which you must plan. Others might be harder to anticipate and mitigate. As we saw in Chapter 13, having a robust culture around governance, risk and compliance will improve your ability to respond if and when you need to.

The impact of disruptive technology

As technology becomes an all-pervasive fact of business life, it's no longer just the preserve of specialist teams or departments. Digital transformation has become an integral part of a CEO's remit, a core element of a company's culture, vision and strategy.

Thomas Siebel, writing in *McKinsey Quarterly*,[6] charts what he calls an 'inversion', with digital change now being led from the top: 'Visionary CEOs, individually, are the engines of massive change that is unprecedented in the history of information technology—possibly unprecedented in the history of commerce.'

Simply put, for Siebel, digital transformation is forcing CEOs to re-think everything about their companies: how products and services are designed, manufactured, sold, delivered and serviced. It's no longer just about competitive advantage, but the difference between having a future – or not. If it's not on a board's agenda, then that agenda is just wrong.

That may sound like a hard ask, but an article by Leor Distenfeld of *Outside Insight*[7] charts three characteristics of business leaders successfully facing the mind-boggling pace of digital transformation. Bear in mind, too, that the prescription starts with having the right mindset.

1. They understand that listening is paramount

Two things here:

Analyse every ounce of data that you have, whether that's third-party industry information or your own customer or client feedback (remember that agile management focus on being client focused?).

---

[6] T. M. Siebel, 'Why digital transformation is now on the CEO's shoulders', McKinsey Digital. Available from www.mckinsey.com/business-functions/mckinsey-digital/our-insights/why-digital-transformation-is-now-on-the-ceos-shoulders [accessed 18 August 2020].

[7] L. Distenfeld, '3 characteristics of the future-proof business executive', Outside Insight. Available from https://outsideinsight.com/insights/3-characteristics-of-the-future-proof-business-executive/ [accessed 18 August 2020].

Listen, also, to your own people. They're a great source of insight too.

2. They are actively engaged in their company's digital transformation

Executive sponsorship matters. Digital transformation is hard, inherently disruptive and often uncomfortable. CEOs need to lend the full weight of their authority to initiatives for them to have even the first chance of working. Awareness is not enough; active engagement is a requirement. This is not just about implementing a technical protocol; it's a matter of alignment with company vision. As Distenfeld notes:

> Future-proof CEOs are diving deep into tactics for innovation and disruption — collecting and analysing as much external data as possible and using it to improve customer experience and remove inefficiencies, assembling C-suite teams and reaching across company and industry borders to share best practices, hiring Chief Information and Chief Digital Officers, and looking increasingly at new technologies.

3. They are seeking new and data-driven methods of creating a sustained competitive advantage

For incumbents within an industry, fast-moving technological innovation can lead to more and more 'digital attackers' eating away at market share. Future-proof executives need to be alert to any rising disruptors potentially infringing on their space.

Cyber security

PwC's annual survey of CEOs looked ahead to 2020 with some trepidation, as their respondents talked about facing a 'rising tide of uncertainty'.[8] Alongside continuing economic uncertainty, the challenges of the skills gap and climate change, one of the top concerns was the need for greater coordination to govern and control the 'unintended and dangerous' consequences of digital technology.

CEO vigilance is certainly needed when it comes to the threat posed by the cyber environment. You will probably be hacked, you may be exposed to ransomware, your business will be disrupted. This is a huge topic (for another book perhaps!) but you must at least have a plan to deal with it.

Look and listen to what is going on around you in the market and learn from it. Formulate a plan, circulate the plan to your team and seek their input. Employ specialists who can audit your current systems, identify gaps in security or operational effectiveness and plug them.

---

[8] PwC, *23rd Global CEO Survey: Navigating the rising tide of uncertainty*. Available from www.pwc.com/gx/en/ceo-survey/2020/reports/pwc-23rd-global-ceo-survey.pdf [accessed 18 August 2020].

15

Exiting with Grace

'Exit, pursued by a bear.'

William Shakespeare,
stage direction, *A Winter's Tale*

WHEN I LEFT my last CEO role, the immediate emotion I felt was one of relief, of a weight being lifted from my shoulders. For the first time in years, I had some space and time to do whatever I wanted. I planned to travel, and to give something back by volunteering for Refugee Rescue, a charity that operates a rescue boat for refugees arriving in the Mediterranean. So, within a month, I found myself on an idyllic Greek island, poised and ready to scramble the boat if we were needed. As we had to be within a 10-minute jog of the boat at all times, this involved plenty of downtime. I spent a lot of it sitting outside a café, writing notes in a notebook for this book. Gradually, though, I began to become restless. This was a massive change of pace from my life as a CEO and, to be honest, I had started to miss being at the centre of things. It was when I started sending emails to myself to check that my sparsely populated inbox was working that I realized that I had started to suffer from what is called 'relevance deprivation', a subject we will discuss further in this chapter.

Whatever the challenges and pressures of being a CEO, it can be hard to let go. But the transition from you to your successor is an important measure of your success while in post. Writing in the

Harvard Business Review,[1] Stanislav Shekshnia and Gry Osnes show that bungling your exit can be bad news for the company and for your successor. Costs in reduced revenues run into millions for companies and billions for the economy as a whole. Not to mention the damage to your personal brand and reputation, which are priceless.

It's incumbent on CEOs, then, to find a way to exit gracefully, to leave your company in the best shape possible and to give your successor the best possible chance of making a go of it. Remember how you felt when you first arrived? Whatever the circumstances of your departure, would you really want unnecessary chaos and uncertainty to make an already massive transition more difficult? Resist the urge to maintain the status quo at all costs. Change is good and the changing of the CEO guard is a particularly good time to ring the changes.

Shekshnia and Osnes's research has identified four basic guidelines for mastering the art of leadership succession and successful CEO exits:

1. Start early

We've said all along that CEOs should look on their tenure as a project with a distinct timeline and milestones. Shekshnia and Osnes agree: CEOs should start planning for their exit as soon as their on-boarding is complete, always on the lookout for potential successors to nurture and mentor.

2. Get help

Succession planning should be a whole board activity, sometimes even delegated to a designated committee. Profiling what's

---

[1] S. Shekshnia and G. Osnes, 'Why the best CEOs are already thinking about their exits', *Harvard Business Review*, 31 October 2019. Available from https://hbr.org/2019/10/why-the-best-ceos-are-already-thinking-about-their-exits [accessed 18 August 2020].

needed in a successor will help to identify whether there are likely internal candidates or whether you'll want to look externally too. Headhunters can be drafted in to look for possible external candidates if needed.

3. Have a retirement plan

It's sometimes hard for incumbent CEOs to consider doing anything else, but that's not realistic. With the length of CEO tenure shrinking, most CEOs will have years of working life ahead of them after they step down. You have to plan a future for yourself outside just one company.

4. Make the break clean

It might be tempting to offer your expertise as a consultant or other advisory role when you step down as CEO. It's a bad idea, bound to lead to conflict with the new CEO, or at least make it more difficult for him or her to take full control and responsibility. Shekshnia and Osnes give the example of an ex-CEO who fell foul of this consultancy trap, which 'not only dealt a strong blow to the company but tarnished my reputation and legacy'. Go for a clean break. Your successor can find other routes to advice and guidance.

Plan for your next step the day you start

The day I started my first CEO role, my leadership coach asked me: 'What's the next job from here?' I had no idea. I hadn't thought about it at all; I'd been too busy preparing for that job. The retort was immediate: 'Well, you had better start thinking about it; you're not going to be here forever.' The fact that so many CEOs don't re-enlist and use what they have learnt in a new CEO role is a shame. What better proving ground for being a CEO than having done it before? Mistakes made, strategies unfulfilled, decisions that might have come back to haunt you... all unavoidable and all learning experiences. My grandfather used to say: 'It's not making a mistake that matters, because making mistakes is part of trying. It's how you deal with the mistake made and ensure you don't make it again. That's the hard part.'

The secret to being a successful CEO is that, while you are doing the best you can to develop your current company, you need to be planning for your next role. As I found out, you have to prepare for your exit the day you walk in. Who knows: you may be out of the door soon enough.

Succession planning is painful, but you have to prepare for it. Do the job to the best of your ability. The aim is to leave the company in a good state, well capitalized, recognized as a market leader, with a clearly enunciated strategy and a well-nuanced succession plan.

Build your profile

Continue to develop your professional networks and make the most of your connections with industry bodies, trade associations and your peers. You need to position yourself as an industry leader outside just your current role.

Be seen as reliable, trustworthy, polite and upfront. Give back and help others; pay it forward. At some point you will need references. You've got to be known as someone who keeps their word, is unflappable, a good leader with a track record of success. This underpinning of trust is crucial. If you lose the trust of the market, by the time you get to the end of your term, you will find it difficult to get another role of similar significance.

Look back at your career, and prepare yourself for the rigours of finding and holding onto that next job. Stay aware of external opportunities. Find out why you weren't considered for any previous roles. Identify any skills gaps that may have contributed and work on them. Take professional advice along the way, and make sure you nurture your relationships with headhunters and other influencers.

Manage your reputation

Around the midpoint of your appointment, you need a reputation check. Contact your PR agency and/or people you have done business with and ask them to grade your reputation, effectively holding a mirror up to you and your performance. It may not be pretty, but it needs to be done regularly in case your tenure is cut short, for whatever reason. Use this information to think about how you will position yourself for that endpoint.

It's also crucial to manage your reputation around your exit. You need to make sure the messaging enhances your reputation and positions you for your next opportunity:

- Get involved in managing the messaging. You will be judged on whether you left the organization in a mess or conducted an orderly transition. The market will come to their own conclusions, based on what your leaving message was.
- Don't allow a message that is open to interpretation. Never say you'll be 'spending more time with family' or similar.
- Recognize that your exit may not entirely be on your terms, since you may be forced to take responsibility for corporate performance or actions that were not of your making.
- Position yourself for the most favourable exit settlement. Understand your worth and negotiate your settlement accordingly.
- Don't threaten to go to the press.
- Don't badmouth the organization in public.
- Leave with grace, so that you can move to your next role with your head held high.

- Support the transition to your successor during the required handover period.

Recognize that it's over – and move on

When the door finally closes on that chapter, your new normality may feel strange: your phone will stop ringing; your email inbox is empty; no one is pulling you aside for that quick chat. Turns out that you weren't as invaluable as you thought: the company is in good hands, the share price is holding steady and the succession plan appears to be holding. This is a good time to take a break and take stock.

So why do you feel so terrible?

Chances are you'll be suffering, like me, from 'relevance deprivation'. It's a term apparently coined by Australian politician Gareth Evans after he stopped being in power. When you lose that power, that sense of being at the centre of things, it can be difficult to find meaning in days that are so much emptier. It can affect your self-worth and even lead to depression. There are, though, some things you can do to manage it.

Re-orient your sense of relevance

One chapter in your career may be over, but that also means a new chapter is opening up. You need to make yourself relevant in new ways. It's time to reinvent yourself.

Open your mind to new possibilities

Whether it's going for another CEO role or changing direction, focus on what you have to offer and how and where you can add value. Rather than replaying past glories, go out and create new ones.

Create a new plan

How do you want to deploy the skills you have? If you've been a CEO, these will be legion. Is there a perfect new CEO role just around the corner? Is this time for a new direction? Believe that you have options. Make a new plan.

When I started to feel like this, I spoke about it to Adriana Giotta. For her, when a career, or a stage of a career, comes to an end, people can feel suddenly invisible: the *persona* they assumed as CEO is not there any more, and it can feel like grief, a real loss. To prevent it is about investing in all the other aspects of one's personality and life, including relationships with children, spouse and friends. This will enable the CEO to not overinflate only one aspect – work and the CEO persona – and to not fuse with it. The persona can become the mask one is aware of wearing in certain circumstances but it is taken off as soon as the role ends: for example, when you are with the children you are the father, not the CEO; when you are with your spouse, you are the husband, not the CEO. But this is easier said than done and needs constant work along the journey. My best advice for any of you feeling like this is to be prepared for it, accept it, allow yourself to grieve – and then let go.

It's time to look to the future.

My Top 10 Biggest CEO Mistakes

'The only real mistake is the one from which you learn nothing.'

Henry Ford

A S YOU'LL HAVE seen throughout the book, I made my fair share of mistakes throughout my career as a CEO, and I've seen other CEOs make them too. Here are my top 10. Hopefully, you'll find that being forearmed really is being forewarned.

1. Feeling that you can't make mistakes

As CEO, you occupy that crucial middle ground between your team and your board and investors. And there are plenty of others, like industry peers and the press, who will always be looking over your shoulder. You may feel a huge internal pressure always to be right.

Wrong!

While you must always look to do the right thing, you simply can't be right all of the time. You'll be faced with mountains of issues needing decisions, often based on imperfect or partial information and a looming deadline. As we saw in Chapter 11, unless you want to risk missing the boat, you might need to trust your instincts based on the best information you can muster and just go for it. You won't be right 100% of the time, but you will always learn something for next time.

2. Failing to understand the spectrum of mistakes

There will be a whole spectrum of mistakes to be made in your dealings with people, both internal and external. You will trust the wrong people and question the motives of those who only seek to help.

There will be occasions when you just don't know which way to turn and you become paralysed by analysis, so that, when you are finally galvanized to take action, the issue will have changed or the opportunity lost. At that point, you need to dig into your wells of experience and knowledge, seek input from those equipped to give it, make a decision and accept that it won't always be the best – something you might realize with the benefit of hindsight, a wonderful thing.

3. Feeling that you have to be perfect

Unfortunately, perfection is ephemeral and hard to achieve on a daily basis. Not setting a high standard or accepting mediocrity is unacceptable, but so is setting the bar so high that nothing gets decided or done, as the organization strives to produce the impossible. Perfection can, so often, be the enemy of the good.

4. Being too keen to make an impact from Day 1

We've seen that the first 100 days of any CEO tenure are important, but that doesn't mean that you should try to do too much too soon. In fact, this can be dangerous and can lead to a multiplicity of additional mistakes. Take the time to learn what you need to know, where the gaps in your knowledge are and how to fix them. Only once you understand what you have on your plate can you start to make informed decisions and effect the changes needed.

5. Being swayed by the people around you

It's tempting to be swayed by the sometimes forceful voices and opinions that will swirl around you from everyone from employees and your board to investors, well-wishers and those who may have more nefarious reasons for giving you a 'steer'.

Taking too much notice of too many, often conflicting, views can lead to analysis paralysis. When you are under fire, take a step back and reflect. Trust your training and that of those closest to you.

6. Not trusting your gut

You should be more evolved than that. When you don't trust your gut, you get hurt; when you override that 'this doesn't feel right' sensation, you are giving up millions of years of survival evolution, even if you can't always put your finger on why. Trust your gut. It will more often be right than wrong!

7. Feeling you must always be making an impact

Allow yourself the time and space to watch the results of things that you put in place. Constantly making changes to agreed strategies and processes is like trimming sails when there's no wind; it might make you look busy, but gets you nowhere and, ultimately, can make you appear indecisive.

8. Allowing yourself to get whipsawed

The demands of the CEO role are such that there are never enough hours in a day, a week or even a month. You will get pulled from place to place: the phone will ring and demand your immediate attention just as someone else appears at your desk with a crisis, and at the same time there will be a ping announcing an email from a board member requiring urgent clarification on something to do with the AGM. If you don't take a disciplined approach to all the issues you face on a daily basis, you will be overwhelmed.

Learn to prioritize and delegate. Allow yourself time to consider options, get second opinions and seek counsel. You need to stand strong above the mayhem of daily operations and look out over the organization in its entirety, intervening where you can make a positive difference and leaving others to do the jobs you have entrusted to them.

9. Being too 'hands-off'

It's vital for your sanity – and the morale of your team – to demonstrate trust in them by not micro-managing, but there are times when you really do need to get involved. Pick your time carefully, but don't leave it so late that your team will think you either don't care or don't want to learn.

I thought my real estate management team could do their jobs without my oversight; after all, they had been managing the properties for years, and there didn't seem to be too many issues. However, my lack of engagement with them for the first three months of my appointment made them think I didn't regard them as important, and allowed some problems to emerge. Remedial action was necessary, which needed to be more drastic than if I'd been course correcting – more gently – all along. My team's perception of me went from 'you don't care' to 'you're micro-managing' overnight. Not helpful. Set the tone early on.

10. Being too 'hands-on'!

There is little to be gained by micro-managing, or appearing to micro-manage, your teams. Team members should be the subject matter experts, or be in the process of gaining that expertise. They will only be able to achieve their full potential if trusted to do their jobs.

If you take that from them, you also add more work to your already overcrowded work day. You won't be doing your job better as a result and you probably won't be doing theirs effectively.

What should you have done?

Picked up a copy of *Three Peaks Leadership* as part of your pre-appointment preparation and read it from cover to cover!